The Obscenity Laws

THE OBSCENITY LAWS

A Report by the Working Party set up by a Conference convened by the Chairman of the Arts Council of Great Britain

WITH A FOREWORD BY
JOHN MONTGOMERIE

ANDRE DEUTSCH

FIRST PUBLISHED 1969 BY
ANDRE DEUTSCH LIMITED
105 GREAT RUSSELL STREET
LONDON WC1

PRINTED IN GREAT BRITAIN BY
TONBRIDGE PRINTERS LTD
TONBRIDGE KENT
233 96204 2

Contents

The Report

INTRODUCTORY

The Origins of the Working Party 11
Procedure and evidence 11

REPORT

The Acts as they stand 14
The purpose behind the law 15
Does obscenity corrupt? 16
Unforeseen applications of the Acts 19
Violence 20
The Conundrum 23
The Acts as interpreted 24
What do we want? 26
The question of *mores* 28
Respect for the law 30
The phantom crime 30
Law and morality 32
Sex taboos 33

CONCLUSIONS

Conclusions 35

Appendices

(A) Draft of the Working Party's Obscene Publications (Repeals and Amendment) Bill 38
(B) The question of reform 42
(C) The Composition of the Working Party 44
(D) Summaries of discussions with:
I The Lord Annan, O.B.E., D.LITT., D.U. 45
II Mr C. Lewis Hawser, Q.C. 45
III Mr Norbert Lynton 46
IV The Rev. David Sheppard 49

V Mr John Trevelyan, O.B.E. 50
VI A distinguished Legal Witness 51

(E) Written statements from:
I Dr G. B. Barker, M.B., B.Ch., D.P.M. 54
II Mr A. Gooch, LL.B. 61
III Mr J. D. Halloran, B.SC. (ECON.) 65
IV Professor R. M. Jackson, J.P., LL.D., F.B.A. 71
V Mr Thomas Joy, F.R.S.A. 79
VI Miss Margaret Miles, B.A. 80
VII National Union of Students 81
VIII Dr Anthony Storr, M.R.C.P., D.P.M. 82
IX Mr Jean Straker 84
IX(a) Obscene Publications (Amendment) Bill 97
X Mr David Tribe 99
XI Mr Keith Wedmore, M.A., LL.B. (Cantab) 105
XII Mr R. J. Werry, C.B.E., B.SC. 107

(F) Documents
I Text of laws indirectly affecting obscenity 109
II Denmark's legislation concerning pornography 116
III Paper from the Danish Forensic Medicine Council to the Danish Penal Code Council 120

Foreword

It was a fascinating experience for me to sit on this Working Party because my views, and those of many other members of the Working Party, changed gradually as we listened to the evidence and discussed the points which emerged.

At the beginning of the exercise I had the same reactions as some of our critics – 'Isn't there enough of sex and violence in literature and the arts already?'; 'Do you want the filthy stuff found in Soho bookshops freely sold over the counter everywhere?'; 'The law may be a bit unsatisfactory but isn't that better than opening the flood-gates?'; 'Isn't it sensible to try to improve the law rather than to recommend the politically unattainable repeal?'. I was definitely a 'reform' man rather than a 'repeal' man. The Reform Sub-Committee produced a draft bill embodying fifteen different points of reform. I was sorry to see it go, but I was fully convinced that to expatiate on reform would only dilute the case for repeal. I hope that the Report and its supporting evidence will explain why after nine months' study we came unanimously to the view which we did. At any rate I will let it speak for itself and not try to go over the ground again.

I should explain the position of the Arts Council, particularly of Lord Goodman, since the obscene anonymous letters arrived on his desk rather than mine. In June of 1968, after the verdict in the *Last Exit* case, the Arts Council was concerned for the protection of authors and artists and convened a Conference of organisations concerned with the arts to consider the problems. That Conference resolved to set up a working party and the Arts Council provided accommodation and secretarial facilities for it. Lord Goodman was not a member of the Working Party and only one member of the Arts Council, Professor Frank Kermode, was on it. Three other persons, including myself, were nominated by the Arts Council. The Working Party produced an entirely independent report which represents the view of the members of the Working Party and cannot even be regarded as the official view of the organisations which were represented on it. Before the Report was referred back to the Conference it was supplied to members of the Arts Council and I had the privilege of presenting it to the Council where it was the subject of lively discussion. The Council agreed to inform the Conference that it regarded the issues discussed in the Report as important in their social implications and in their relation to the arts. The Council considered that the Report showed the need for investigation into these issues particularly as far as they concern the artist and his work and his relations to the public. The Conference adopted the Report with three dissentients and decided that it should be sent to the Home Secretary.

The Home Secretary, while not giving much hope of legislation in this parliament, has stated that he himself would welcome further study and I sincerely hope that this will be undertaken at an early date. For myself, I would confidently prophesy that no Royal Commission could find a satisfactory definition of 'obscenity' or be able to draw an intelligible line between what is acceptable and what is not acceptable. Nor do I believe that such a Commission could find any evidence that anyone has been corrupted or become depraved by pornography. Giving full weight to the differences between Scandinavians and Anglo-Saxons, I think that a Royal Commission might well come up with the same conclusions as the Danes and decide that the Obscene Publications Acts may do more harm than good.

Our Report predictably received a mixed response from the press. The *Guardian* thought that the case had never been better stated; while the *Telegraph* thought we ought to have worked on it harder. *The Times* agreed that the law could never be satisfactory, but nevertheless favoured its retention. The *People* argued strongly that the law should be kept as it is. The *Scotsman* was favourable, the *Glasgow Herald* highly critical. The Bishop of Woolwich in the *New Christian* thought we had done a noble service and produced a lucidly argued analysis: the *Tablet,* on the other hand, doubted whether the Working Party had done much homework at all.

No doubt the debate will continue for some time to come – and the crucial point which in my view emerges is: whether the burden of proof is upon us to show that the law ought to be changed, or whether any restriction on freedom of speech needs to be justified by showing that in its absence some definite harm will result. I take my stand firmly on the latter proposition.

JOHN MONTGOMERIE

The Obscene Publications Acts
The Report of the Working Party

Introductory

1. THE ORIGINS OF THE WORKING PARTY. A Conference was convened by the Chairman of the Arts Council on 6 June, 1968 to which 150 individuals were invited, and 22 organisations, considered to be concerned about legal sanctions which had been or could be used against literature, drama and visual arts, were invited to send representatives. In fact about 90 people attended including representatives of 21 organisations.

2. The Conference passed a resolution in the following terms:

> 'This Conference, convened by the Arts Council of Great Britain, wishes to resolve that a Working Party be set up to investigate the working of the Obscene Publications Acts 1959 and 1964, and other relevant Acts, with special reference to literature, drama and the visual arts, and to consider such changes including the repeal of any such Acts as in their opinion shall be expedient, and to report back to this Conference with such recommendations as they deem necessary.'

The Conference nominated certain bodies which should be represented on the Working Party and gave the Working Party the right to co-opt any other members if they so wished. The Conference expressed the wish that the Working Party should co-opt a representative of the live theatre. The ultimate composition of the Working Party and the bodies which they represent is set out at Appendix C to this report.

3. PROCEDURE AND EVIDENCE. The Conference required us to consider the case for abolition of obscenity laws as well as any improvements to the existing laws which we thought fit to recommend. We therefore divided ourselves into two sub-

committees, one to consider reforms to the existing laws and one to consider the case for repeal. Oral evidence was considered by the Working Party as a whole.

4. The following members of the Arts Council staff attended meetings of the Working Party:

Mr Eric W. White, C.B.E. (Literature Director)
Mr Charles Osborne (Assistant Literature Director)
Mr N. V. Linklater (Deputy Drama Director)
Mr Dennis Andrews (Assistant Drama Director)
Mrs F. L. Jenkins (Literature Assistant)

The Art Director was kept informed of proceedings.

5. Appreciating that the Working Party consisted largely of people concerned with the production side of literature and the arts, we endeavoured to obtain evidence from as wide a field as possible, including people and bodies who might represent other points of view. For this reason we invited written comments, inserted an advertisement in *The Times* personal column and specifically invited a number of people to attend and give evidence. We are very grateful to those who gave oral evidence before us or who submitted written papers and we append to this report as Appendix D brief summaries of our discussions with witnesses; as Appendix E, copies of some of the written statements which we received and, as Appendix F, copies of some of the documentary evidence which was available to us.

6. The sub-committee investigating possibilities of reform examined at some length substantive and procedural defects in the present law and indeed attempted to draft a Bill as an alternative to the existing Acts. But, although some peripheral improvements were devized,* the central problems remained obdurate and it was not found possible to construct a law addressed to so nebulous a goal that circumvented the objections set out later in this Report. Juries would still be faced with an unanswerable conundrum, defendants would still find themselves on trial for an unpredictable crime, judges would still be floundering in a sea of indeterminate paradox and little good therefore could accrue to the law's repute.

In fact, it is true to say that the Working Party began its task

* See Appendix B.

with the knowledge that reform would be less controversial than repeal and therefore with the hope that it might be feasible. That we have come to the opposite conclusion is certainly not the result of prior intention but of examining the problem with as open a mind as possible.

7. It should be added that, although a recommendation for repeal was agreed by the Working Party *nem. con.* and was also the personal preference of most witnesses, doubts had been expressed as to whether the recommendation, however valid its reasoning, might not seem too radical for Parliamentary acceptance. Against this, it is fortunately true that Parliament does not always wait upon public opinion; sometimes it leads it. There have been notable examples in recent years.

But more important still, the task laid upon the Working Party was to recommend what ought to be done, not to recommend on the basis of conjecture what Parliament might agree to do. It would be irresponsible to recommend what ought not to be done simply on the conjectural grounds that this is what Parliament might wish to do. And what ought not to be done, in the Working Party's view, is to leave legislation against obscenity on the statute book, for reasons which are set out in the following report from the sub-committee on repeal as finally amended and adopted by the Working Party.

Report On Obscenity Laws

THE ACTS AS THEY STAND

The Obscene Publications Act, 1959, though it introduced many improvements, was unable to overcome the hard basic fact that no two people can be counted upon to agree what is or is not obscene. A wholly subjective adjective is no very promising foundation for a law which should command maximum acceptance and be capable of some objective application.

However, an attempt at definition had to be made and after much head-searching the bill was drafted on the basis of a formula originated in 1868 which defined obscenity as 'a tendency to deprave and corrupt'.*

No definition has ever been offered to show what was meant by depravity and corruption. 'Nobody,' Mr Hawser, Q.C. told the Working Party,† 'knows what this means.' It was clear that one inscrutable phrase had been resorted to in explanation of another.

Lord Goodman, who has considerable legal experience in these fields, has described the resulting situation as 'a total nonsense . . . juries were expected to decide difficult questions of ethical and philosophical value; but the original purpose of a jury was to decide facts, not make decisions involving opinions.'‡

The Working Party had therefore to ask themselves whether there was any way of avoiding this total nonsense if it be really true that the nation requires (and nobody knows that it does) obscenity to be ranked as a crime rather than as a matter for social censure. It is social censure and public opinion that we normally look to to regulate the evolution of private *mores* and if, instead, we insist that this continuing process be translated and crystallized

* The relevant paragraph in full is as follows:
'. . . an article shall be deemed to be obscene if its effect or (where the article comprises two or more distinct items) the effect of any one of its items is, if taken as a whole, such as to tend to deprave and corrupt persons who are likely, having regard to all relevant circumstances, to read, see or hear the matter contained or embodied in it.'

† Recorder of Salisbury.

‡ Reported in the *Daily Telegraph,* 7 August, 1968.

into a penal law, we have only ourselves to blame when judges and Parliamentary draughtsmen fail to convert an inescapably subjective word like obscene, whose interpretation varies not only from person to person but from year to year, into an acceptably objective law capable of reasonably consistent application. That they can only offer us question-begging periphrasis should be no surprise because we have left them without guidance as to what is intended to be achieved. They cannot say what they mean because they do not know what they mean, and they do not know what they mean because we cannot tell them what we mean them to mean.

'Obscenity,' said one distinguished legal witness,* 'is incapable of objective definition and is therefore an unsatisfactory subject for the criminal law.'

In short, if we ask silly questions, we must expect silly answers.

THE PURPOSE BEHIND THE LAW

Before committing ourselves, however, to abolition of the obscenity laws, it is worth examining sympathetically what is or could reasonably be their purpose.

It is not to protect people from being shocked. Some time in our lives we have all been shocked and, even though we may not have liked it, do not feel ourselves to be sensibly the worse for it and sometimes know ourselves to be all the better. Indeed to shock has always been one of the beneficent social functions of art, an inevitable by-product of the fresh vision which characterises a good artist and which helps to protect society from inertia and paralysis.

This no doubt is why few people would wish the arts to be emasculated to a point where they could shock nobody. The demand comes only at the idea of shocking a 'significant' minority. But if freedom from shock is to be elevated into a civic right, then this right must be guaranteed to everybody. An insignificant minority (if such a line could ever be drawn or ascertained) is as much entitled to protection as a larger number. To accept this

* Owing to his official position, which is relevant to this whole subject, he can only be quoted anonymously.

reductio ad absurdum would mean that nothing could be published which might shock anybody.

In conformity with this view, Mr Justice Stable, when trying *The Philanderer* case in 1956, went out of his way to warn the jury that the words 'to deprave and corrupt' must not be construed as 'to shock and disgust', which is not a criminal offence.* This point was emphasised again by the present Lord Chancellor four years later in the *Lady Chatterley* trial.

DOES OBSCENITY CORRUPT?

There is no ground, therefore, for the fairly common misapprehension that mere protection from shock or disgust is the objective of obscenity laws.

Indeed, as they stand, they would appear to aim at much bigger fish; nothing less than anti-social influences in the arts. But is this a practicable objective? It is certainly a fish that we have found as hard to identify as the monster of Loch Ness. All we can say for certain is that speculations abound and contradict each other; verifiable fact is virtually non-existent. 'The supposed depravity and corruption produced by obscene articles is a matter of conjecture,' said Professor R. M. Jackson.† 'No hard evidence can be put forward, for nobody can demonstrate that anybody has ever been depraved or corrupted by a particular obscene article. A decision that an article would have such a tendency is based entirely upon opinion unsupported by verifiable facts.'

This view was largely confirmed by experts from the psychiatric and social sciences. 'There is,' said Dr G. B. Barker,‡ 'absolutely no solid evidence to my knowledge that any person has ever been depraved or corrupted solely by the effect of literature or exposure to the arts.'

And Mr Halloran,§ despite a heartfelt plea that his own organisation should be more handsomely endowed, could go no further than express a hope that, given more money, it might be

* Unless the law has been changed by Lord Justice Salmon's ruling in the Court of Appeal, 31 July, 1968. See p. 24, 26 and 28.

† Downing Professor of the Laws of England in the University of Cambridge.

‡ Medical Administrator and Consultant Psychiatrist at a large London psychiatric hospital.

§ Director of the Centre for Mass Communications Research, Leicester University.

possible, in a decade or two, to establish whether any causal connection existed between erotica and sexual offences. However, his excellent summary of researches by better-provided colleagues abroad, who also seemed to have secured no such evidence, tended to undermine even this qualified hope.

But whatever the future may hold, at this moment of time Professor Jackson's view seems to be a simple statement of fact. It is further endorsed by the Psychiatric Department of the Council of Forensic Medicine of Denmark, whose report to the Danish Government in 1965 was a contributory factor to the repeal of obscenity laws in that country.

After a survey of researches all over the world the Council states 'that, as far as the Council is aware, no scientific experiments exist which can lay a basis for the assumption that pornography or "obscene" pictures and films contribute to the committing of sexual offences by normal adults or young people. On the basis of psychiatric and child-psychiatric experience it can neither be assumed that sexual leanings, the development of personality, and the ordinary attitude to sex and to ethical-sexual norms either in children or adults, can be detrimentally affected by the means in question (pornographic literature, pictures and films). It is doubtful whether these can have a beneficial effect on sexually shy, neurotic people, but it cannot be completely ruled out. This statement holds good regardless of whether the pornographic writings, pictures, etc. are of normal or sexually perverted content.'

Elsewhere the Report says, 'It is commonly known in medical science, that sexual leanings are fixed at an early age, probably around 5–6 years old,* and are in any case completely established by the end of puberty. It is therefore hardly likely that the reading of "obscene" writings or the sight of films, etc. will change the sexual leanings of an adult person.'

'Obscenity,' said the witness already quoted on p. 15, 'does not corrupt, though it may appeal to the corrupt. The rationale for the existing law does not exist.'

Mr John Trevelyan† declared frankly his personal belief that

* Dr Barker emphasized the same point; so does another eminent psychiatrist, Dr Anthony Storr.

† Secretary of the British Board of Film Censors.

erotic films depraved nobody and that his own censorings were largely directed to protecting the film-makers, who employed him, from possible legal action so far as it could be guessed in advance.

Said Mr Gooch, Magistrates' Chief Clerk to the Marlborough Street Court, 'I have never heard any evidence being called to show that any depravity or corruption has in fact been induced by a work. It is always left for the Court to infer.'

In the light of all this it becomes less mysterious that nobody appears to find *in himself* an example of a person actually depraved by erotica. Nobody seems even to have met such a person. Far more people claim to have seen a ghost. So discussion tends to centre on a hypothetical, unencountered 'them' in contrast to incorruptible 'us'. This perhaps is why in 1962* the Courts established that no amount of exposure to pornography can deprave a policeman. He is indissolubly one of us. This blanket certificate may well be deserved; but, if so, should it not be issued also to barristers, bakers, bankers, billiard-markers, brokers, bellmen and every other known category? On the evidence available it would seem so.

It should be added that the preceding paragraph is subject to one discoverable exception. The Rev. David Sheppard (now Bishop of Woolwich), had hinted in the witness-box when *Last Exit to Brooklyn* was on trial that he himself may have been depraved by it† and was good enough to meet us. In the event he impressed us deeply but not as an awful example of depravity. On the contrary he left us with the feeling that, if this was a depraved man, then society had little to fear and much to gain by his multiplication. Certainly here was no very persuasive argument for repression.

He himself reminded us that repression could also be psychologically injurious and confessed himself unable to suggest any formula that Parliament could sensibly adopt. His own view of sexual propriety was based on his own (perhaps controversial) interpretation of a passage in the Sermon on the Mount but, although he claimed the right to proselytize this view, he rejected,

* R. v. *Clayton and Halsey*.

† At the same trial it seemed that Sir Basil Blackwell had also found himself 'corrupted' by reading the book at the age of 79 but only in a rather special sense.

as a disestablishment man, any claim to impose it by law on his fellow-citizens; a self-denying ordinance which the Working Party fully endorses and seeks to emulate.

UNFORESEEN APPLICATIONS OF THE ACTS

So far, this Report has dealt with obscenity in its popular or dictionary sense as related to sex. But, although the Acts of 1959 and 1964 make no mention of drugs or of violence, the courts have already extended the field to include them; not surprisingly since the Acts do define obscenity as anything tending to deprave or corrupt; i.e. anything with guessably anti-social results.

It cannot therefore be reasonably excluded that all manner of fresh offences may also be seen sooner or later to fall within the scope of these Acts, as indeed they undoubtedly do. Is there no tendency to corrupt in a handbook for pickpockets, such as Dickens incorporated in *Oliver Twist*? What about the multitudinous thrillers that offer guidance to murderers and ingenious advice on the disposal of corpses? Or the 'Westerns' whose hero is pre-eminent in violence and slaughter?

And if the depiction on celluloid of sadistic behaviour and its gruesome consequences tends to deprave and corrupt, what about a similar depiction on canvas? Goya might escape on the grounds of artistic merit but the same claim could hardly be sustained on behalf of many pictures displaying the horrors of the Crucifixion.

Nor is there any reason why artists and novelists should remain fair game while journalists remain exempt. In time, if the present law on obscenity persists, it will be the press's turn to find it used against them; and not only the less reputable section of it that thrives on detailed accounts of mayhem, ancient and modern, of robbery, fraud, rape, assorted violence and orgies, all providing invaluable instruction for the aspiring criminal, but also the more austere newspapers and magazines that expose the bestialities of war with documentary photographs.

And it certainly cannot be long before the temperance societies become aware of the weapon that has come to their hand. It is hard to see how a court that had convicted a serious novelist, however dubiously, of incitement to drug-taking* could fail to

* *Cain's Book* by Alexander Trocchi, 1963.

condemn the publication, in every possible mass medium, of propaganda – for gain – openly inciting citizens to take alcohol, of which the proven effects can be unbridled aggression, sudden death or maiming of innocent strangers, illness and impaired working competence for the addict and immeasurable domestic tragedy. Here the anti-social effects are not speculative but undisputed. Every advertisement for gin unquestionably contravenes the Obscenity Acts.

Nor is even the spread of ideas safe from threat, though this was certainly not Parliament's intention. But few people would deny that ideas can corrupt more powerfully than a drawing of pubic hair and the Acts could certainly be invoked against many a Hyde Park speaker as legitimately as against Mr Dine – or Mr Trocchi, who wrote very neutrally about drug-takers.

To put it no higher, therefore, there is ground for reasonable fear that these Acts, because of their inevitable inadequacy of definition, will degenerate into a miscellaneous hold-all unrelated to their original intention or to good sense. The abuse of the Vagrancy Acts is an ominous precedent.

Opinions may differ as to whether the unforeseen additions that have so far extended the scope of the Acts as a result of common law embroidery are desirable and whether still further extensions on the lines envisaged above should be accepted. But most people would agree that matters of such fundamental importance should not be left to the hazard of a single court judgment but should properly be determined by a sovereign Parliament.

VIOLENCE

A special word should be said on the subject of violence.

It is true that the Working Party were able to find no evidence of a kind that either lawyers or social scientists could accept to prove that crimes of violence any more than crimes of sex were induced by literature and the other arts. Nevertheless, we had some sympathy when Mr Trevelyan, who agreed in regarding erotica as socially harmless, confessed to feeling 'perhaps not quite so sure' about the depiction of violence. This could well be due simply to the fact that most people, including Mr Trevelyan and members of the Working Party, don't like violence and do like sex. But a majority must resist the temptation to prohibit whatever it happens to dislike and be guided instead by social consequences if they are calculable. Only on that principle could the homosexual laws have been made more humane.

Certainly a suspicion of personal prejudice would be roused if we opposed the legal prohibition of erotica on the ground that evidence of calculable social harm was lacking and yet sought to prohibit the depiction of violence even though its effects likewise cannot be shown to result in the practice of violence. After all, a different Working Party on the same subject but appointed, say, by the Ministry of Defence might note in themselves a completely opposite bias. They could hardly ignore the threat to national survival if British pugnacity were eroded by a taboo on the portrayal of violence and would logically view with alarm any signs that Britain was becoming seriously converted to Christianity, with its associated doctrine of non-violence.

It may well be subconsciously for some such reason as this that there happens to have been only one solitary prosecution under the Obscenity Acts where a defendant has been charged with publishing an article conducive to violence.* And it is perhaps significant that neutralist Sweden, although more tolerant than this country in matters of sex, is far less lenient on the subject of violence.

In any case, if we were led to suspect that our own misgivings about the depiction of violence, which the Courts do not appear to share, are rooted more in prejudice than in reason, this suspicion was reinforced when Dr Barker, with plenty of clinical experience behind him, declared 'Much of the reading of these patients consists of comic books and stories that abound in sadistic material. I would never dream of banning such books from the hospital however and we have no evidence that it has caused any episodes of violence, and indeed, it is as much a part of their way of life as "Romances" are to others. It has a cathartic effect and withdrawal would cause tension . . . I personally would allow

* *D.P.P.* v. *A. & B.C. Chewing Gum Ltd.,* who were convicted for issuing, inside packets of bubble-gum, cards picturing atomic atrocities likely to deprave their juvenile customers.

both so-called pornographic and sadistic literature in prisons. I believe it would relieve and not provoke tension.'

Even in the less committed view of Mr Halloran, the most that could be said at present by way of tentative conclusion, as far as mass media were concerned, was that heavy exposure over a long period to the portrayal of violence (e.g. prize-fights and wrestling matches?) might have the ultimate effect of 'desensitizing' people to violence or possibly reinforcing a predisposition where values were unformed. However he made clear that this was no more than speculation and certainly did not suggest that the ubiquitous atmosphere of violence which we have all been brought up to accept as our native background could even begin to be transformed by the Obscenity Acts or other available laws which, perhaps for that very reason, are virtually never invoked against it.

A further argument was put to us by Mr Keith Wedmore, barrister and co-author of a relevant pamphlet issued by the Society of Friends.† 'I arrive at the same conclusion' (i.e. the repeal of the Obscenity Laws) 'for the . . . reason that a story is a story, and the distinction is well understood; that children (and immature people) have their real behaviour influenced by their actual relationships; that, except for the grossly inadequate minority for whose special needs we must not try and frame our rules, we do not copy art in life; we accept it for what it is, a copy *of* life, or an expression of its desires and fantasies. Whatever nebulous case there may be for the argument that a particular incident in a book or on the screen set off a particular crime or incident – significantly most usually suggested in relation to suicide – there is a slightly stronger suggestion that we sleep and even behave better after witnessing scenes that "get it out of our system". But frankly my own group knew of little impressive evidence either way; so that on our impressions you would be justified in not having censorship on the simple ground that it serves no demonstrable purpose.'

This cathartic view (as it is sometimes called) that the depiction of violence exorcises rather than induces is held by many psychiatric investigators, like Dr Barker, and questioned by some others; but neither side have been able to offer 'demonstrable'

† *Towards a Quaker View of Sex.* Mr Wedmore is also Clerk of the Quaker Penal Affairs Committee.

proof. And bad though it is for us to expect juries to give their opinion on opinions, it is still worse when the opinions of presumed experts are known to be divided.

THE CONUNDRUM

Yet this is expressly what the Obscenity Acts expect; and not only in respect of violence. For jurors are not only enjoined to decide what may or may not tend to deprave and corrupt with no possible guidance except from sociologists who either disagree with each other or candidly confess that there is no knowing; but their verdict must also enshrine their judgment on the equally imponderable question of artistic merit. Here they can be supplied with guidance – or additional confusion – by so-called experts,* who may also be divided against each other.

Moreover, juries are even required to assess the '*number*' of persons likely to be depraved (whatever the word may mean) and whether they amount to a 'significant' proportion or an insignificant one. Apparently it is fair enough and perfectly acceptable that a man should deprave a few people and corrupt a few more; but not too many. It is for the jury to decide how many is too many.

Nor is this the end of the juror's dilemma. Worse awaits him. Having decided (on what grounds who can guess?) that an article might spread 'depravity' among a 'significant' number of people and yet contain elements of artistic merit in doses large enough to be construed as for 'the public good', he must then ask himself whether an ounce of depravity-spreading is more or less potent than an ounce of artistic merit, tot up the ounces of depravity and of art that he deems to be present in the disputed article and base his verdict on this egregious equation.

It is perhaps not surprising that the suggestion has been made that only jurors with A-levels should be allowed to wrestle with such problems; on the other hand it is to be doubted whether anybody with even a single O-level would solemnly set himself to make the attempt except under inescapable duress.

Now it was because Judge Rogers had apparently felt himself

* Not that history confirms the existence of any such animal. Most unfamiliar art, written, aural or visual, has been broadly condemned by its contemporaries.

unable to recite this conundrum from the Bench with a straight face that his direction to the Jury was faulted by a Court of Appeal.* Said Lord Justice Salmon, 'In effect he (Judge Rogers) threw them (the jury) in at the deep end of Section 4 and left them to sink or swim in its dark waters.' Dark was a well-chosen adjective. But whether the conundrum was really a potential life-belt in disguise or a dead-weight for ensuring permanent submersion, the second view seems to have been held by the Director of Public Prosecutions, whose letter to the defendants was quoted in all fairness by the appellate Judge: 'If you find – as I am afraid you will – that this is a most unhelpful letter, it is not because I wish to be unhelpful but because I get no help from the Act.' Lord Justice Salmon's comment was that his court had 'considerable sympathy with that attitude.'

THE ACTS AS INTERPRETED

It is inevitable that sooner or later, when statutes are impracticable or vacuous, common law rushes in to fill the vacuum. Lord Justice Salmon declared that it was 'often unwise for the judge to attempt to improve upon or refine the definition'. Nevertheless his own valour outrunning his discretion, he himself later supplied a gloss of far-reaching importance and consequence in an attempt to disentangle the legal imbroglio described above.

He laid it down that corruption 'may be (1) to induce erotic desires of a heterosexual kind, or (2) to promote homosexuality or other sexual perversions, or (3) drug-taking, or (4) brutal violence.'

The thing that immediately strikes us is that a law which was dangerously vague has now become dangerously specific. Let us examine the ruling.

In the first place, by thus specifying four classes of offence, the judge's ruling has at least served to remind us of an important distinction between the last pair and the first; namely that, drug-taking and brutal violence being recognised crimes, incitement to commit them is also a crime, punishable under Common Law and under statutes quite other than the Obscenity

* R. v. *Calder & Boyars Ltd*, 31 July, 1968: the *Last Exit to Brooklyn* case.

Acts. Insofar as an article amounts to an incitement to crime, the Obscenity Acts are redundant. Since society already has such protection as law can afford, it is clearly superfluous to include these two matters within the scope of the Obscenity Acts by stretching the word 'obscene' to embrace them; an interpretation that neither man-in-the-street nor lexicographer would readily recognise.

It should perhaps be noted however that under the Obscenity Acts a new and, one would have thought, self-contradictory concept has been introduced; that of *unintentional* incitement to crime (or, as will be seen later, even non-crime). Normally intention is of the essence. Lack of it is a legitimate plea open to the defence. But under the Act of 1959 it is irrelevant. It cannot even be raised on the defendant's behalf. The mere *depiction* of crime (or even non-crime) regardless of intention is proscribed as incitement and sufficient ground for conviction (e.g. Trocchi's case).

Here, in the matter of admissible evidence, there does indeed appear to be an important innovation but one that could hardly be acclaimed as an improvement.*

Let us be clear therefore that incitements (unless unintentional) to drug-taking or violence would remain punishable offences even if the Obscenity Acts should be repealed.

Secondly, the first two items in the judge's list are in a very different category. Erotic desire is not a crime; and it is to be hoped for all our sakes that it does not become one. Nor, since

* It is hard not to conclude that the object of this refinement, especially in the context of the Acts, is not so much the prevention of crime as protection against the *presumed* threat to the moral character of one citizen by another; i.e. the concept of law as a *custos morum*. This threat is of course no more than presumable, even in relation to 'the occasional fifteen-year-old maladjusted delinquent'. Indeed, since hardcore pornography became legally available in Denmark at prices that even the poorest delinquent can afford, the incidence of sexual crime has dropped as a result (or coincidence) by the astonishing figure of 25 per cent. (This figure has been confirmed by the Press Counsellor of the Royal Danish Embassy in London). Which may well be a point notched up for the 'cathartic' school of psychiatrists. But in any case nobody (openly) demands that the arts should be tailored, in Mr Justice Stable's phrase, to 'the misfits of society'. The normal assumption of law and of public opinion is that the citizen can stand up to the inroads of experience upon his pristine innocence, that he alone is the final custodian of his own character and his private morals and that it is neither a feasible nor a desirable function of the State to replace him as custodian.

1967, is private homosexuality between consenting adults; nor is onanism, if that be one of the other unnamed 'perversions'. Yet, according to the judge's ruling it is now a heavily punishable crime to 'induce' these particular non-crimes. It is now a criminal offence for us to incite each other towards practices or even sensations that are themselves perfectly innocent according to the law.

Clearly we are now landed in a paradoxical situation that would no doubt have delighted W. S. Gilbert but cannot fail to concern those of us who regard not only justice but the law's repute as of some importance.

Its full absurdity may be illustrated by a hypothetical example. If a young woman were to admit in Court that listening to a record of 'The Valkyrie' had induced in her 'erotic desires' (a by no means uncommon experience), she would not be guilty of a crime but the young man who thoughtlessly played it to her would be. So too of course would the company who issued the recording, provided that the jury considered that a 'significant number' of music-lovers were receptive to the aphrodisiac element in Wagner, which, as an army of musical experts would be ready to testify, is not only present but hard to miss.

But, it may be said, the commonsense of jurors would step in to rescue the law in so extreme a case. Possibly so, though it is not very desirable to rely on juries to override a strictly valid legal direction from the judge. And what about cases that are less extreme, less demonstrably nonsensical?

It is true that Lord Justice Salmon, perhaps subconsciously uneasy at his own ruling, later appears to have undermined it.

'The jury,' he said, 'must set the standards of what is acceptable, of what is for the public good in the age in which we live.'

These may be disarming and sedative words but their practical effect is only to throw juries back into the deep end again because this is an exhortation which implicitly renounces the possibility of useful legal guidance.

WHAT DO WE WANT?

No blame can attach to Lord Justice Salmon for failing to illuminate the dark and turgid waters in which jurors are condemned to struggle; nor to the Director of Public Prosecutions who was too shrewd to plunge in beside them. His lordship, like the Parliamentary draughtsmen, was in the position of a coachman invited to drive us to an address that we are unable to specify. Nobody knows exactly where we want to go. All we seem to know is where we don't want to go. We don't want to fetch up in a situation where it is a crime to shock or even disgust.* We don't want to curtail the vital rights of free speech. We don't want repression for the sake of repression. We don't want to arraign bad taste or bad manners, for these are matters for social reprobation, not for penal law. We don't want to hobble the arts; still less to constrain them to a level fit for – in Mr Trevelyan's phrase – 'the occasional fifteen-year-old maladjusted delinquent'.

So perhaps what we do want, suggested Lord Justice Salmon in desperation, is to equate ordinary sexual desire with depravity and to regard as criminal anything that conduces to it.

Obviously, as soon as such a proposition is expressed in words, it is seen for something too silly to be accepted by reasonable men and women. Nevertheless, his lordship may well have been right in guessing that this very idea, albeit in a shape so blurred and inchoate as to obscure its own extravagance, was present in the minds of those who in 1959 still considered some form of legislation against obscenity as self-evidently necessary. If no more than this is indeed the underlying assumption of the Acts, the judge performed a further service in calling attention to the fact so vividly.

Of course it cannot be denied that surviving pockets of society do still regard sex, alone among the appetites, as an unfortunately necessary evil to be forever deprecated and discouraged and fit only to be whispered about. Indeed this attitude was reflected by a Treasury Counsel. (Their advice to the D.P.P. as to the wisdom of launching a trial is usually decisive.) He was asked privately what guided him in recommending a book for prosecution. He replied – in confidence, so he must remain anonymous – that the test he used was whether the book had made him feel randy. 'Entirely subjective,' he said, 'but what else is there?'

Exactly: what else indeed?

* See p. 16.

Yet three comments suggest themselves. (1) It is doubtful whether this gentleman's revulsion at randiness is shared by a 'significant number' of Her Majesty's subjects and at least arguable whether it ought to be. (2) Even accepting that more randiness may lead to more love-making, we must then decide whether that is an activity to be contained at a desirable level and, if so, (harder still) at what level. And (3), if human randiness is a social evil and the object of obscenity laws is to extirpate it, then the task of formulating effective legislation for the purpose may as well be abandoned at once as, to say the least of it, unpromising.

However extravagant all this may seem, it does begin to appear that the case for legislation against obscenity rests, ultimately and solely, not upon any hard factual analysis of anti-social consequences but on a vague generalised residual apprehension, which Lord Justice Salmon's ruling has crystallized, to the effect that sexual desire is a form of depravity and should be repressed by law.

The Working Party accepts neither proposition and cannot regard them as healthy; still less for the public good, in the age in which we live.

THE QUESTION OF MORES

This whole tangled web of anomalies that we have examined, threatening as it does both the law's repute and the individual's expectation of justice, seems to follow inevitably upon any attempt to convert non-conformity with current *mores* into a penal offence.

This is the core of the matter; in the last analysis Obscenity Laws are really about conformity and *mores*. That is why Lord Justice Salmon,* after a valiant effort to find a more solid basis for them, had finally to retreat from the attempt and admit that all we could, in practice, expect from a jury was their opinion of 'what is acceptable . . . *in the age in which we live*'. That is another way of saying 'what is not shocking to contemporary *mores*' and its effect is directly to contradict Mr Justice Stable's warning to the jury; 'The charge is *not* that the tendency of the book is to shock and disgust.'†

* See p. 26.

† R. v. *Secker & Warburg*, 1956. During the Chatterley case in 1960 the present Lord Chancellor emphasised the same point.

Obviously depravity and corruption, far graver words, are not subject merely to the age in which we live. Much could shock Victorians that does not shock us but what could deprave them only because they were Victorians? Depravity and corruption are not, presumably, 'acceptable' in one age and unacceptable in another. This variable applies only to what shocks or disgusts. Perhaps it is only because legislation making it a crime for us to shock each other would almost certainly be rejected that the more ominous phrase 'deprave and corrupt' was introduced instead. Nor is it only Lord Justice Salmon who devalues these two elusive words by defining them merely as what is unacceptable in the age in which we live. He is genuinely reflecting the existing practice in court, where inevitably juries decide the issue not on an assessment of evil consequences which they have no means of judging but by the criterion of current *mores*.

The use of such a criterion, which turns a Court of Law into a *custos morum* and dates from the days of the Puritans, is, of course, not unique in English law, as Professor Jackson reminded us. 'We have to recognise,' he said, 'that the purpose of some offences is to support and maintain various conceptions of acceptable conduct.' And later, when discussing the case of *Shaw* v. *D.P.P.* 1962, he added, 'The worst feature of the case was, however, the vigorous assertion by Lord Simonds that the court is *custos morum* of the people, for which of course there is judicial authority from the 17th century onwards. It is, however, a somewhat astonishing doctrine these days to say that in the last resort the way we can behave, the things we can read, look at, hear and presumably enjoy, are subject to Big Brother, wigged and gowned on the judicial bench. The decision has been much criticised by lawyers.'

Arguments in the same sense, if less forcibly expressed, will be found *passim* through this Report.

In any case, for better or worse, it is important to recognise that, officially, since July 1968, juries are expected to stabilize *mores* at their current point of evolution (if they can ascertain it) by punishing anyone with different standards that may therefore shock or disgust a significant number of people. Alternatively or additionally, they may punish anyone whose work *may* result (proof is not required) in the legally innocent sensation of erotic desire or, of course, in the condoning of legally innocent homosexual practices.

If Lord Justice Salmon had been able to emulate the reticence of Judge Rogers and the D.P.P., which was not very easy for him in a Court of Appeal, he would not have floodlit for us the lack of admissible motive behind the Acts and hence the essential impracticability of such legislation.

RESPECT FOR THE LAW

The threat to the law's repute is a matter that has seriously concerned the Working Party. That threat is present when a law:

(1) is so unintelligible as to baffle even Directors of Public Prosecution and to bereave judges of the power to direct juries in terms that can be seen to be sensible;

(2) is so obscure in intention that even a morally innocent transgressor cannot ascertain in advance whether he will have transgressed it or not, so that, although ignorance of the law is not permitted to him as a defence, it is imposed upon him as a fact by the very nature of the law;

(3) is aimed to prevent hypothetical social evils that the prosecution is not required to prove or even to specify and whose very existence as a consequence of the offence is unproven and probably unprovable;

(4) is a virtual vacuum waiting to be filled by the divergent opinions of juries as to what the law might have meant if it had been able to express itself; thus reducing beyond the point of toleration the prospect of reasonably consistent application and therefore increasing the element of mere hazard imposed upon defendants.*

THE PHANTOM CRIME

These conditions tend not only to bring the law into disrepute

* Most laws of course are to some degree susceptible to inconsistency of application – a matter which is believed to be under consideration by the Law Commission – but the question of degree is all-important and the Obscenity Laws by their nature are probably the most flagrant in the unpredictability of their operation.

but also set justice at risk. Whereas any man who robs a cash-box knows (or could have ascertained) that he is committing a crime, a man who writes a book may have no intimation that he is at work on a criminal offence till the moment he finds himself condemned to prison for perhaps three years and to payment of a fine of unlimited amount and of prohibitive costs. Which is a little late. He cannot inform himself in advance because the only issue to be resolved in court is, in essence, whether this particular jury's unbuttressed opinion of what is innocuous agrees with the writer's opinion. If it does not, then the writer has committed a crime. As it might be in roulette, he wins on 'evens' and loses on 'odds'.

Nor do courts normally condemn a man on the mere unproven suspicion of unintentional evil-doing. But this entire Act is itself based on no more than the mere unproven suspicion of unintentional evil-doing.

It is an Act under which a man is punished not simply for what he does (e.g. writing a book) but for the unproven consequences of what he does (i.e. corrupting a number of people) and, still more essentially, for the unpredictable consequences of these consequences (e.g. a case of rape committed by a corrupted reader). He is therefore being punished in reality as an unwitting accessory before the fact to a crime that may never be committed. On the face of it, this would appear to be going rather too far.

A man can at least know in his heart whether he is guilty of embezzling; he cannot possibly know whether he is guilty of depraving and corrupting. Nor for that matter can the judge or jury that condemn him; because 'nobody knows what this means'. And if it means some threat to society, nobody can specify what or even adduce evidence that it really exists. Only personal opinion remains. And when judge and jury, who should be making public judgments, are reduced to making private ones, then law has degenerated into censorship.

The present situation is that judge, jury, witnesses, prosecution and defendant are all operating in limbo with no meaningful statute to help them and are themselves condemned to the use of words and phrases that beg whatever question may be the unrevealed purpose of the trial. In short, they are all engaged in the trial of a phantom crime.

LAW AND MORALITY

It has been argued that the basic difficulty is one of framing a practicable law with the aim not of directly countering crime (like embezzlement) or curbing the socially irresponsible (like laws against dangerous driving) but of responding to an indefinite, generalised apprehension of impaired morality. However, even assuming such legislation to be feasible, is it desirable?

Morality is a portmanteau word with a vast heterogeneous capacity. It is used to embrace moral concepts, habits of mind, standards of behaviour, religious dogmas, social *mores* and even manners. None of these categories commands unanimous assent or practice 'in the age in which we live'. Morality evolves and the community straggles along with it. But neither stragglers nor leaders should be condemned or harassed, especially by the law. Morality, as Mr Sheppard maintains, must not be imposed. When Shaw claimed to be, like Ibsen, an immoral playwright, he was proclaiming his own moral compulsion as an artist to question the morality of the age in which he lived. That, it may well be thought, is a socially valuable service which should not be baulked.

Even if it were desirable to embalm morality as it happens to be in the age in which we live, does repressive legislation do the trick and what happens without it? The only concrete experiment in our time has been made in Denmark where the laws against obscenity in literature were repealed in June, 1967. There had already been a flourishing but expensive underground market for pornography which increased substantially for a few months after legislation. And then it slumped to a level well below the period before repeal, in spite even of slashed prices, leaving a number of successful publishers in the genre either bankrupt or struggling to build up a more respectable list of publications. The show was no longer a peepshow.

It is significant that, when interest in now *legal* written pornography declined, sales of still *illegal* pictorial pornography increased. Fruit would appear to be more marketable when forbidden.* (Cf., the Prohibition Laws in America, which led to an enormous increase in the habit of hard drinking.)

* Encouraged by the success of his experiment, the Minister of Justice is shortly to introduce a Bill extending it to include the visual media, with the sole restriction that the *display* in streets of pictorial erotica shall be constrained.

Whether this experiment be conclusive or not, it must at least be of some reassurance to those who fear that without legislative repression pornography must flourish; and is relevant to the question, Does the Working Party view with equanimity an enveloping flood of pornography in the wake of repeal?

There are four answers:

(1) that no such thing may result, unless human nature in Britain differs radically from what it is in Denmark;

(2) that even now the supply of pornography appears to be quite adequate to meet the demand since nobody in quest of it has any difficulty in satisfying his needs despite the busy and costly apparatus of Customs control and the wholesale destruction of imports;

(3) that the Working Party, like judges and juries, have no means, outside their varying individual prejudices or guesses, of assessing how harmful to society erotica may be, so long as evidence is completely lacking to the effect that it is harmful at all; and

(4) that the harm would need to be both indisputable and very dire indeed before it could be judged to outweigh the evils and anomalies inherent in the Acts we have been asked to examine.

In short, we cannot recommend that Parliament should prescribe for the body politic an inept and disabling cure in order to forestall an imagined malady.

SEX TABOOS

Moreover, there is a sensible contemporary feeling that in general the area of all legislation has increased, is increasing and ought to be diminished; and that, subject to demonstrably anti-social consequences, it is wiser to permit than to repress. The so-called permissive society may have its casualties; the repressive society almost certainly had a great deal more. Repressed sexuality can be toxic both to the individual and to society. Repression can deprave and corrupt.*

Is this high price worth paying (and only part of the price at that) in an attempt to constrain our sexual proclivities? Certainly it would be a mistake to imagine that fifty years ago sources of titillation were lacking; indeed, they were probably more plentiful, though scarcely recognisable as such to us today. Even the glimpse of a stockinged ankle was titillant at the turn of the century. The first line of chorus girls to appear bare-legged was an aphrodisiac spectacle – and ceased to be so within a twelvemonth. Custom and acceptance are the great anti-aphrodisiacs. Nothing could be more antiseptic sexually than a nudist colony. There the almost essential peepshow quality has been eliminated, with predictable results.

This is why the puritan in D. H. Lawrence was shocked and angry that subjects should 'become dirty (and slyly cherished) only because of futile attempts to suppress them. Words derive their deliciously vile connotations from restraints rather than from use.'†

By advocating suppression it is likely that those who fear the influence of erotica are shooting into their own goal. Conversely, those who defend erotic sensations as, at the lowest, a natural pleasure should mistrust the permissive society for reducing the area of opportunity. They would however probably regard as more than adequate compensation the fact that a sense of guilt in regard to our sexual inclinations has been correspondingly reduced and a great deal of psychological illness prevented, as well as a great deal of social hypocrisy.

* 'Our knowledge of the Victorians shows that the outward rigid morality of the era hid a shambles of repressions, conflict and neurosis and the flagrant existence of a second world of illicit sexuality on the part of men, and much cruelty, humiliation and disregard for humanity in the treatment of women . . . In my experience I have never met any patient whose condition was caused by "exposure to sexuality", but I have met innumerable examples of ignorance, fear and ideas of guilt causing much neurotic illness and unhappiness.' – Dr G. B. Barker.

† Walter Gelhorn in *Restraints on Book Reading,* published by the American Library Association.

Conclusions

We may now sum up the main reasons which have led the Working Party to make the recommendations which follow for repeal of the Obscene Publications Acts:

(1) It is not for the State to prohibit private citizens from choosing what they may or may not enjoy in literature or art unless there were incontrovertible evidence that the result would be injurious to society. There is no such evidence.

(2) No crystal ball can tell us dogmatically whether more or less pornography would result from Repeal but in any case there is a complete absence of evidence to suggest that sex in the arts, even when aphrodisiac in intention, has criminal or anti-social repercussions.

(3) Though it is sometimes conjectured with no indisputable evidence that heavy and prolonged exposure to the portrayal of violence may not only reflect but also influence the standards of society, violence has been ubiquitous in the art, literature and Press of the civilised world for so long that censorship must by now be recognised as a totally inadequate weapon to combat it. Indeed laws available for the purpose including the Obscenity Acts are virtually never even invoked against it.

(4) Since judges have to work in what is in effect a legal vacuum, the prosecution of an occasional book – usually the wrong one – often succeeds only in bringing the law in to disrepute, without effectively preventing the distribution even of that book.

(5) The very objective of the law is not even established, let alone identified in concrete meaningful terms that could command acceptance. Although judges emphasise that an article cannot be condemned because it shocks or disgusts, in practice that is precisely what happens, since juries have no other criterion to guide them.

(6) It is impossible to devise a definition of obscenity that does

not beg the question or a rational procedure for weighing depravity and corruption against artistic merit and the 'public good'.

(7) When juries and defendants are without a comprehensible definition of the crime alleged, the defendant is left at the mercy of a personal opinion; which is a system of censorship rather than a system of law.

(8) It is intolerable that a man should be criminally punished for an action that he has no means of ascertaining in advance is criminal.

(9) Incitement to criminal behaviour is sufficiently covered by the ordinary law of incitement. To that extent the Obscenity Acts are redundant. Insofar as they add the concept of a mere unintentional tendency toward crime as a punishable offence they are to be deplored.

(10) It is an affront both to legal and common sense that incitement to a non-crime should be punishable as a crime; and worse when this doctrine is extended to a mere tendency.

(11) No encouragement should be given to the concept of the State as *custos morum* with its corollary that merely to shock is a criminal offence.

(12) The proper sanction for breaches of taste or non-conformity with current *mores* should be social reprobation and not penal legislation.

The foregoing analysis has led the Working Party firmly to the conclusion that the laws against obscenity, while constituting a danger to the innocent private individual, provide no serious benefit to the public. The basic problem of founding a law that can be accepted on so subjective a concept as obscenity appears to be insuperable. Any formula of definition must be doomed to beg the question, so there can be little hope of formulating alternative legislation with more than peripheral improvements.

The Working Party therefore recommends that the Obscene Publications Acts of 1959 and 1964 should be repealed and should not be replaced for a trial period of five years or even at the expiration of five years from that date unless Parliament should otherwise determine. The Theatres Act 1968 should be brought into line.

It also recommends that certain other relevant Acts should be amended or repealed. Many of these have been or could be used as a basis for indirect censorship and contain words such as 'indecent' and 'profane' which are no more capable of definition than 'obscene' but which may be used to circumvent any need to establish harmful consequences.*

We recognise, however, that it is reasonable to protect individuals who may be affronted by offensive displays or behaviour in public places. There are various Acts dealing with this, for which we would substitute a single section so that there should be no overlapping.

We would not seek to interfere with the existing arrangements under which the British Board of Film Censors classifies films into various categories. Television is not in practice affected by the Obscenity Acts and we are content that the B.B.C. and I.T.A. should be left to conduct their programmes on their own responsibility, with such regard as they see fit to pay to ascertainable public opinion.

We would leave intact the Children and Young Persons (Harmful Publications) Act 1955.

A draft Bill follows at Appendix A setting out the changes in the law which would give effect to the above recommendations.

* An example of this is the prosecution of paintings and pictures under the Vagrancy Acts 1824 and 1838, under which convictions have been obtained on the ground that the pictures were 'indecent' (which is something less than 'obscene') and no defence on the ground of artistic merit was possible.

Appendix A

Draft of The Working Party's Obscene Publications (Repeals and Amendment) Bill

EXPLANATORY MEMORANDUM

The Purpose of the Bill is to repeal the Obscene Publications Acts 1959 and 1964 and to amend the provisions of various Acts which may be used in order indirectly to achieve the same objects as those Acts.

ARRANGEMENT OF CLAUSES

(1) ABOLITION OF CERTAIN OFFENCES
(2) REPEALS
(3) AMENDMENT OF THE POST OFFICE ACT 1953
(4) OFFENSIVE BEHAVIOUR
(5) CITATION COMMENCEMENT AND EXTENT

A

BILL

TO

A.D. 1969

Repeal the Obscene Publications Acts 1959 and 1964 and to amend various correlated Acts

BE IT ENACTED by the Queen's Most Excellent Majesty, by and with the advice and consent of the Lords Spiritual and Temporal, and Commons, in this present Parliament assembled, and by the authority of the same, as follows:

Abolition of certain offences

1. (1) No person shall be proceeded against for an offence at common law in respect of the publication of an article where it is of the essence of the offence that the article was obscene, indecent, offensive, disgusting or injurious to morality or that the persons against whom such proceedings would be brought have conspired to publish such an article.

(2) No person shall be proceeded against under any local Act or by-law where it is of the essence of the offence that the person has published an article which was obscene, indecent, offensive, disgusting or injurious to morality.

Repeals

2. The Acts referred to in the first column of the Schedule hereto are hereby repealed to the extent set out in the third column of the said Schedule.

Amendment of the Post Office Act 1953

3. No proceedings shall be brought under section 11(1)(*b*) of the Post Office Act 1953 unless the packet is addressed to a person who

(*a*) has not solicited it or is unaware of the nature of its contents; and

(*b*) is offended thereby.

Offensive behaviour

4. Any person who in any street, road, highway or other public place exposes or exhibits or delivers to any person any indecent article or behaves in an indecent manner so as to offend persons who read or see the article or witness the behaviour in question shall be liable on summary conviction to a fine not exceeding £50 or on a second or further conviction to a fine not exceeding £100 or two months' imprisonment or both.

Citation commencement and extent

5. (1) This Act may be cited as the Obscene Publications (Repeals and Amendment) Act.

(2) This Act shall come into operation on the expiration of one month beginning with the date of the passing thereof and shall continue in force unless at the expiration of five years from that date Parliament should otherwise determine.

(3) This Act shall not extend to Scotland or Northern Ireland.

Schedule

REPEALS

Chapter	*Short title*	*Extent of repeal*
5 Geo. 4 c.83	Vagrancy Act 1824	In section 4 the words 'Every person wilfully exposing to view in any street, road, highway or public place any obscene

		print, picture or other indecent exhibition'.
1 & 2 Vict. c. 38	Vagrancy Act 1838	Section 2.
10 & 11 Vict. c. 89	Town Police Clauses Act 1847	In section 28 the words 'Every person who publicly offers for sale or distribution or exhibits to public view any profane, indecent or obscene book, paper, print, drawing, painting or representation, or sings any profane or obscene song or ballad, or uses any profane or obscene language'.
39 & 40 Vict. c. 36	Customs Consolidation Act 1876	In section 42 the words 'Indecent or obscene prints, paintings, photographs, books, cards, lithographic or other engravings or any other indecent or obscene articles'.
52 & 53 Vict. c. 18	The Indecent Advertisements Act 1889	The whole Act.
7 & 8 Eliz. 2 c. 66	The Obscene Publications Act 1959	The whole Act.
12 & 13 Eliz. 2 c. 74	The Obscene Publications Act 1964	The whole Act.

14 & 15 Eliz. 2 c. 80	Criminal Justice Act 1967	Section 25.
15 & 16 Eliz. 2 c. 54	Theatres Act 1968	Sections 2 and 3.

Appendix B

The Question of Reform

(1) It transpired from the Judgment of the Court of Appeal in the *Last Exit to Brooklyn* case that it was the duty of a judge to explain to a jury at some length that 'obscene' did not mean obscene at all in the sense in which the jury would understand it. They are therefore at the beginning of the summing up to be told that they have to decide whether the book is obscene but 'obscene' does not mean obscene but something else. This is likely to throw them into considerable confusion at the outset. We considered therefore whether some word like 'harmful' could be substituted for 'obscene'.

(2) On the other hand, the statutory definition of obscenity as something that has a tendency to deprave and corrupt might lead to an extension of the obscenity laws to cover anything tending to promote anti-social behaviour of any sort. We considered how to keep the law within limits.

(3) We thought that the jury would find some difficulty in interpreting the 'significant proportion' of the potential readers who were supposed to be likely to be corrupted but could not improve on this phrase.

(4) We found difficulty about the question of time limits for prosecution, since the existing protection relates to the date of the act of publication which is the subject of the prosecution. The protection ought obviously to be given in respect of books which have been available to the public for more than a certain period, which we thought should be a year.

(5) We found a number of anomalies in the proceedings for forfeiture and we thought that all prosecutions should be authorised by the D.P.P. or a constable and that in all cases there should be a right of trial by jury.

(6) We thought that there should be some protection of original drawings and paintings from destruction.

(7) Most important of all we thought that the paramountcy of freedom for literature and the arts required that the burden should be firmly placed on the prosecution of proving not only that the publication had harmful tendencies but that those harmful tendencies outweighed any merits to be found in the publication. But we were aware that this would be as hard to establish as it is to refute.

(8) We were also concerned at the abuse of other Acts such as the Vagrancy Acts 1824 and 1838, the Town Police Clauses Act 1847, the Indecent Advertisements Act 1889 and the Post Offices Act 1953 in order to operate an indirect form of censorship and with the powers of the customs authorities to impose their own standards in this field.

The sub-committee's draft Bill would help to obviate some of these defects, but they were still left with one fundamental defect in the Acts, namely that prosecution for obscenity involved putting before a jury who might be illiterate or semi-literate the task of weighing up allegedly harmful tendencies upon which they had no expert guidance and no expert knowledge themselves against the merits, if any, of the article in question upon which they were entitled to have the help of expert witnesses but upon which they themselves would be in most cases quite unqualified to judge. The reform sub-committee considered various schemes for improving this situation, such as independent assessors to assist the judge and jury or the recommendation of some specialist committee as a prerequisite for proceedings, but all such schemes have their own disadvantages and objections and the sub-committee was not able to produce any satisfactory alternative to trial by jury.

Appendix C
The Composition of the Working Party

Chairman:
Mr John Montgomerie

Members:
Nominated by

The Arts Council of Great Britain	Prof. Frank Kermode Mr John Mortimer, Q.C. Mr R. G. Davis-Poynter
The Booksellers Association	Mr T. A. Joy
The Defence of Literature and the Arts Society	Mr John Calder
The English Centre of International P.E.N.	Miss Kathleen Nott
The Institute of Contemporary Arts	Mrs Dorothy Morland
The League of Dramatists	Mr Benn W. Levy, M.B.E.
The Library Association	Mr T. E. Callander
The National Book League	Mr J. E. Morpurgo Mr Clifford Simmons
The National Council for Civil Liberties	Mr Tony Smythe
The Publishers Association	Mr R. H. Code-Holland, C.B.E. Mr F. J. Warburg
The Society of Authors	Mr C. R. Hewitt (C. H. Rolph)
The Society of Young Publishers	Mr Howard Loxton
The Writers Guild of Great Britain	Mr Ronald Harwood

Co-opted to represent the live theatre — Mr William Gaskill

Appendix D.i

Report on Discussion with The Lord Annan O.B.E., D.Litt., D.U.,

Provost of University College, London

Lord Annan was firmly against the idea of constraining the arts to a level fit for the maladjusted fifteen-year-old. Assessments of the anti-social effects of these things upon an individual could never be more than speculative because human behaviour was the result not of one but of a multiplicity of causes. He thought that the important criterion was whether it could be shown that any work was likely to corrupt and deprave, and not whether it would give offence to certain virtuous people.

He did not think, as Mr Trevelyan had tentatively suggested, that intention could be a feasible factor in determining what might or might not be permissible, as many excellent books had been written by authors whose avowed intention was to make money. Conversely, the highest intentions could produce bad books. In any case it was difficult to argue that the author's 'intention' had any direct bearing on the excellence or worthlessness of a work of art. The criteria of 'art' or 'good taste' were equally difficult to apply.

He agreed that the legislature might well reject total abolition of the obscenity laws, which he personally favoured, but reminded us that this did not mean that the common sense point of view would not be accepted sooner or later and he cited the long years of campaigning that had preceded the abolition of capital punishment and the reform of the homosexual laws.

Appendix D.ii

Report on Discussion with Mr C. Lewis Hawser Q.C.

Mr Lewis Hawser outlined the existing legal sanctions dealing with obscenity and indecency and drew attention to the distinction between statute law and common law. He discussed 5 questions that arose from the legal point of view in connection with publication etc. and gave his views on them as follows:

(1) Common law offences of obscenity and indecency should be abolished.

(2) 'Public exhibition' should be more closely defined, restricting it to cases where there was offence to the public at large.

(3) Defendants should be given the right to trial by jury in seizure cases.

(4) The police should not have power to prosecute without the permission of the D.P.P. or Attorney General.

(5) A tribunal or specialist jury should be used in cases brought under the Obscene Publications Acts. (He considered that a two-stage trial would be cumbersome and expensive.)

Mr Hawser was in favour of all relevant sanctions being consolidated in one Act.

Appendix D.iii
Report on Discussion with Mr Norbert Lynton

Head of Department at Chelsea School of Art, Art Critic to the Guardian, *member of the Art Council's Art Panel*

(1) Mr Lynton said that his contact with the Obscenity Laws had been limited to the Stass Paraskos case in Leeds in December 1966, when he had been called as one of eleven expert witnesses. The Stipendiary Magistrate in that case had considered it to be his duty to assess obscenity by the standards of the 'man in the street', and the prosecution won its case against Mr Paraskos. The prosecution repeatedly questioned the expert witnesses as to whether they would be offended if they saw people in the street

behaving as the people in the picture appeared to be doing; the magistrates seemed to be impressed by this and to share the prosecution's view that there could be no distinction at the level of morality between a representation and a real act.

(2) Mr Lynton said that art had not so far been widely prosecuted. In the Jim Dine case, when pictures had been removed by the police from a gallery in Davies Street, W.1, the gallery owner was charged and convicted under the Vagrancy Acts. Mr Lynton had been surprised to hear of the Hockney affair. Seizure by Customs officials was discussed, and Mr Lynton suggested that imports valued at under £5 should not be subject to seizure. The Chairman said that Customs officials seemed to have a fairly rigid set of rules, which they applied in a rule of thumb way.

(3) Much of the greatest art of all periods was directly concerned with sex and violence. Mr Lynton suggested that the visual arts were vulnerable under the Obscene Publications Acts in ways in which literature is not, partly because of the relatively low state of education and general awareness in this field. The ordinary man has little or no contact with the visual arts, yet it is, in Lord Parker's phrase, 'the modesty of the ordinary man' that was to be the measure of whether or not an offence had been committed. Yet, at the same time, there appears to be a special potency credited to images, in that objects and events quite frequently referred to or even described in detail in books were not permitted delineation. The Jim Dine works had been elegant graffiti; repetitive in subject matter but of high merit for the manner in which they were executed. Mr Lynton said that he had never encountered a work of art of quality that could also be held to 'deprave and corrupt'.

(4) Censorship of works of art was discussed; Mr Smythe mentioned the banning by the local authorities in Croydon of an art exhibition in a municipal hall because it included paintings of the war in Vietnam, and the banning by London Transport from their buses of a poster that was a work of art. The Literature Director said that in the Stass Paraskos case the local authority had been involved because that exhibition too had been in a municipal building. Mr Lynton said that Stass Paraskos had been

a student and a teacher at the Leeds School of Art; they had borrowed works from him for an exhibition in the college, up two flights of stairs, which was open to the public. The exhibition had been opened by a civic dignitary some weeks before a policeman went in. It was open to question whether the Education Officer concerned should have been charged, not Stass Paraskos. Mr Lynton said that in Bradford paintings had been removed from an Arts Council exhibition because they showed pubic hair; truth was apparently held to be corrupting while lies were not. The history of such events shows unvaryingly that it is never titillating works that are accused of being obscene but rather those in which the accusers' expectations of titillation were disappointed. Mr Hewitt's suggestion was discussed that there should be some sort of tribunal – or national or regional committee – to whom a defendant or court could refer a work of art. The Chairman pointed out that a tribunal could judge artistic merit, but not whether the work was depraving or corrupting. Mr Levy said that the suggestion implied an acceptance of the present law in principle.

(5) Mr Lynton stressed that under section 3 of the Obscene Publications Act 1959 a work found to be obscene could be destroyed. In the case of the books this would mean the destruction of an edition; other editions, proof copies and the original manuscript would be likely to survive. In the case of a unique work of art such destruction would be total and final. Mr Calder said that paintings (like manuscripts) were unique; while it might be argued that the artist should be prevented from exposing his work to public view, there should be no power to order its destruction. It was considered that no committee would ever order destruction, and that if an artist were refused the right to further expose his work that would be penalty enough. (Mr Warburg said that the notoriety gained by such a work would ensure a ready market for it.)

(6) Mr Lynton said that a distinction might be drawn between a work that was exhibited in a way that related to the enjoyment of art, and a work that was exhibited in the way of mass dissemination through magazines, etc. In the Stass Paraskos case no charge had been made for entry to the exhibition, so that in theory it was

open to everybody, but in fact the 'man in the street' opted to be no longer in the street if he went inside the building to see it. (Mr Loxton pointed out that strip club posters were in the street.)

(7) The question of sentencing works of art to 'life imprisonment' was discussed, possibly in the British Museum, the National Gallery and/or the Tate Gallery. It was realised that if no banned works (even picture postcards) were ever to be destroyed, the collection would become enormous, and judging which works should be kept would be invidious and unacceptable to the artist. Mr Calder said that objects (as opposed to publications) might remain in the possession of the artist, but be banned from sale, exposure or reproduction for a set period and or until some person applied when circumstances changed for the ban to be discharged on artistic or sociological grounds.

(8) Mr Harwood queried whether the obscenity was in exhibiting a picture, or in painting it. The Chairman said that before 1964 the purchaser of a work had to be proved to have been corrupted by it.

Appendix D.iv
Report on Discussion with The Rev. David Sheppard

Bishop of Woolwich and Warden of the Mayflower Family Centre, Canning Town, London, E.16

The Rev. David Sheppard said that when he had appeared as a witness for the prosecution in the *Last Exit* case, he had said in court that he 'had not been unscathed' by reading the book. He considered that if he had read it at an earlier stage in his development it might have encouraged him to explore the world it described, which could have been very damaging.

He considered that books did influence people, particularly when their reading was unbalanced or restricted. Books provided vicarious experience; they could heighten the loneliness of people who found it difficult to have relationships, and they could sap people's moral responsibility. He believed that some people gloried in violence, and that books could encourage violence. He wanted some check to exist but he did not want heavy censorship and feared that the 'swingback' might be more dangerous than the permissive society. He did not think that society could pretend that it believed in no censorship at all: there was no escape from the need to put up a fence at certain points. Society needed to debate where the fence should be put up. But he confessed himself unable to see how the right kind of legal fence could be devised and called attention to the danger of repression.

Appendix D.v
Report on Discussion with Mr John Trevelyan, O.B.E.

Secretary of the British Board of Film Censors

Mr Trevelyan said the British Board of Film Censors aimed at reflecting the contemporary attitudes of the intelligent public. He described shots passed recently which would not have been let through ten years ago, but maintained that a large percentage of the population was still surprisingly puritanical.

He very much hoped that the Working Party would succeed in the difficult task of finding a meaningful formula for obscenity, as this would facilitate his own task in as much as one of his functions was to protect film producers from legal action. At present, like the Courts themselves, he was necessarily operating in limbo.

He made the usual distinction between sex and violence, and did not himself consider that sex films were in the least likely to have anti-social consequences unless they involved elements of sexual sadism or some other perversions. But he was less sure about displays of violence, which could possibly produce emulation in the occasional fifteen-year-old maladjusted delinquent.

Appendix D.vi
Report on Discussion with a distinguished Legal Witness

This witness said that as it was impossible to define 'obscenity' which was an amorphous concept that changed with the times, his view was that all obscenity laws should be abolished. This, however, was probably an impractical proposal in present circumstances, but some improvement could be achieved.

In particular, the 'fringe' laws should be abolished. He considered that their powers of seizure were exercised by Customs officials too freely and with gross unfairness, and that it was wrong that travellers entering the country from whom material was seized had no redress.

He appreciated that it might be necessary to exercise control over the import of material for trade or gain, and thought that the seizure of such material as was considered to be obscene under existing sanctions should be argued before a jury at Assizes or Quarter Sessions, with an option open to the defendant to ask for summary proceedings (small booksellers or other importers might not wish to go to the expense of a full-scale trial; but an importer wanting to defend his action should not be at the mercy of a magistrate).

He said that he favoured:

(*a*) the abolition of all legal sanctions other than the Obscene Publications Acts of 1959 and 1964 against literature, drama and the visual arts;

(*b*) the restriction of the powers of seizure of H.M. Customs and Excise to material being brought into the U.K. for trade or gain (abolition of all censorship not a practical proposition at present);

(*c*) legislation giving the right to opt for either trial by jury or by summary proceedings before a magistrate to defendants against whom action was taken by:

  (i) H.M. Customs and Excise under the Customs Consolidation Act, 1876, Section 42.

  (ii) The Postmaster-General under the Post Office Act 1953, Section 11.

A member of the Working Party suggested that the onus of proof of obscenity in a seizure case should be on H.M. Customs and Excise, who should bear the cost if they lost the case. The witness welcomed this suggestion, and said it would remove an incentive to search passengers' belongings, without affecting the scrutiny of consignments of goods at docks, etc. imported for gain.

Considering the phrase 'tendency to corrupt', he said that while obscene publications might attract a corrupt person, they could not of themselves corrupt. He thought that any attempt to define obscenity or to draw distinctions between the influence of publications, etc. pertaining to sex, drugs and violence would be sterile. He recognised, however, that many people thought that they could distinguish, and that literature, etc. depicting violence could exert an influence.

A member said that sadism in literature was the subject of a legal sanction not connected with obscenity.

Another member said that the definition of obscenity could be extended beyond the three categories of sex, drugs and violence; tips to criminals in Conan Doyle books could be said to have a tendency to corrupt; information about fraud was given in books and films, and so on. The witness said that he had no wish to extend the existing 'definition' of obscenity: he considered that the conception of obscenity as an offence should be abolished.

The witness summarised his views as follows:

(1) Obscenity does not corrupt, though it may appeal to the corrupt. The rationale for the existing law therefore does not exist.

(2) Obscenity is incapable of objective definition, and is therefore an unsatisfactory subject for the criminal law.

(3) Nevertheless the climate of public opinion is not such as would permit the obscenity laws to be swept out lock, stock and barrel; one can only work for some amelioration.

(4) To this end the fringe laws and by-laws should be abolished, leaving only the Obscene Publications Acts of 1959 and 1964 to cover the field. Necessary Post Office and Customs & Excise powers can be brought within these statutes.

(5) 'Trade or gain' should always be part of the essence of the offence.

(6) Trial should be on indictment unless the defence requests summary trial and the prosecution consents.

(7) Goods seized must be returned within, say, twenty-eight days unless a prosecution is initiated within that period. The burden of proof must always be upon the prosecution.

(8) Penalties should not include destruction of original works, but may include confiscation and preservation until an application for release (which may be made at any time, in the light of changing social conditions) is successful.

(9) The ideal to work for, however, was complete abolition.

Appendix E.i
Comments received from Dr G. B. Barker, M.B., B.Ch., D.P.M.

Medical Administrator and Consultant Psychiatrist at a large London Psychiatric Hospital

(1) THE WORKING OF THE ACTS IN PRACTICE

I have no personal experience of the working of the Acts in practice, except to say that uncertainty about the whole position at the present time has prevented myself and my colleagues and I believe those in another hospital also, from pursuing research into methods of conditioning therapy that would have been useful to patients and interesting and fruitful professionally. This work has been carried out in some hospitals but always with certain difficulties, and the material we require, e.g. the depiction of lesbian relationships, is not easy to obtain. Publicity, at this time also, appears to discourage this type of research, e.g. the publicity afforded to Professor Eysenck in his planned survey of 'common sexual practices of normal people'. If it is true also that Aston University, Birmingham has been discouraged from making a film for use in sex education, then I think that the Acts must be working in a manner not in accordance with their original intent.

(2) OTHER ACTS

This is rather allied in my mind with (1) above, in that as things are at present it would seem that a variety of Acts, By-laws, and other legal sanctions are almost interchangeable for the purpose of administering a policy that may change at any time with the general policy of the 'Authorities'; with changing attitudes of individuals whether magistrates or Ministers, and even with the locality involved.

It seems to me ridiculous that a well-known personality for example had the indignity of a prosecution under the Post Office Act 1953 for 'returning unsolicited material through the mail'.

Even the magistrate was apologetic, but had to administer the law.

It seems to me intolerable that a Brighton magistrate can remark in court on the integrity of expert witnesses from a university and impose fines on a bookseller for an offence that might not even have come to court at all in a different locality.

It is equally wrong that an individual, for example, Sir Cyril Black, however sincere his motives, can force a case into court even against the original rebuff from the Director of Public Prosecutions, merely because of his own particular opinions and standards.

It is wrong that one of the best known booksellers in the country should withdraw from their shelves copies of *Justine* merely because the book was mentioned in the well-known Moors trial. It is wrong that the film censor – so intelligent and enlightened a man – should be so bothered by pubic hair that he had to call a press conference to justify his cutting of 15 seconds from the film *Hugs and Kisses* before it was shown in the West End.

One could continue almost indefinitely with such examples, but I hope I have made the point that laws that appear ridiculous must be bad laws.

(3) EVIDENCE RELATING TO THE EFFECTS OF LITERATURE AND THE ARTS

There is absolutely no solid evidence to my knowledge that any person has ever been depraved or corrupted solely by the effect of literature or exposure to the arts.

Having made such a sweeping and dogmatic statement one is then forced to expand and qualify it.

(*a*) SEX

Sex and nudity are now much more openly portrayed on film and described in literature, and nudity is now accepted, if in context, on the stage.

This would seem to me to be utterly healthy.

Our knowledge of the Victorians shows that the outward rigid morality of the era hid a shambles of repressions, conflict and neurosis and the flagrant existence of a second world of illicit sexuality on the part of men, and much cruelty, humiliation and disregard for humanity in the treatment of women.

In my experience I have never met any patient whose condition was caused by 'exposure to sexuality', but I have met innumerable examples of ignorance, fear and ideas of guilt causing much neurotic illness and unhappiness.

The pattern of responses of an individual to sexuality is formed by very early relationships – certainly before the age of 6 – and a healthy or neurotic reaction follows on this developed pattern.

The opinion that pornographic material for example has played a part in the formation of the character of a delinquent is due largely to the opinion of law enforcers who might find such material in the possession of wrong-doers. This ignores the fact that there can be very few men in this country who have not, at some point in their lives, had access to such material without any apparent deleterious effect whatsoever.

Investigations among teenagers reveal that very few of them gained any sexual knowledge from printed matter and that among 100,000 boys interviewed in one typical American city only 2.1 per cent from the middle and 1.3 per cent from the upper social groups had been influenced by this matter.

Of the same sample, 90.8 per cent and 93 per cent respectively of the two groups had been told about sex by male companions. Parents, school and religious authorities appeared to be remarkably absent.

It is amazing in clinical practice how ignorant apparently 'grown-up' youngsters in early adolescence are about sexual matters. This ignorance covers the whole field of sexual anatomy, the significance of the 'period', venereal disease and contraception.

In gaining knowledge from their peers much use is made of so called pornographic photographs and other material, shown by the older to the younger members of the group and in this way it can only be regarded as educational, although it would clearly be much better if such knowledge could be given more freely by the parents. This is a vicious circle. The inhibitions of one generation prevent the free discussion of sexual matters with the next. Nothing engenders more emotion than the teaching of sexual instruction in schools. If these matters were freely accepted, pornography would lose much of its impact.

A. S. Neill has some interesting things to say in this respect about 'Summerhill', the school that he founded in 1921.

I would state dogmatically that if nudity was accepted completely from the earliest age, there would be far less neurotic unhappiness, and less need for vicarious enjoyments of alternatives to sexuality. It is likely that there would also be less promiscuity, because promiscuity is based upon the neurotic inability to find or to form an adult relationship.

I am not suggesting that everybody should constantly walk about naked in all situations, but that a healthy knowledge and regard for the human body, the loss of repressions connected with guilt about the desire for such knowledge, would produce a person with fewer conflicts and a better organised ego.

In Denmark today, censorship does not exist for those over the age of 16. I believe that the next generation will benefit if the authorities have the courage to continue this policy and I would wish that this could be followed in this country in some manner or other. I would suggest that it is the puritanical pressure groups in this country that cause pornography to flourish. If this pressure ceased then the problem would fall into quite a different perspective.

It is important to dissociate the term 'permissive society' from 'laxity' and to equate it instead with 'intelligent sophistication'. It is the repressive measures of the 'new morality' that perpetuates the problem and drives it underground.

(*b*) VIOLENCE

This is a different problem altogether and it is a pity that sex and violence should be so inextricably mixed and confused in people's minds. Of course they are connected because when emotions run high, violence may not be far away, but this is not the same problem as tackled by the authorities in the matter of censorship. Probably no single theory will ever explain the wide variety of violent behaviour, and one of the problems in dealing with this matter is the natural desire to seek a causation that will fit all the facts and to over-simplify the problem itself.

In my own practice, apart from episodes of psychotic violence and violence due to psychological disturbance I see many patients, particularly young girls, with behaviour disorders, in whom there is a history of violence.

One thing that they invariably have in common is a disturbed background from the earliest years and I have already made the point that it is the earliest years of life that are the most important from the point of view of attaining maturity.

Much of the reading of these patients consists of comic books and stories that abound in sadistic material. I would never dream of banning such books from the hospital however and we have no evidence that it has caused any episodes of violence, and indeed, it is as much a part of their way of life as 'Romances' are to others. It has a cathartic effect and withdrawal would cause tension. It is a matter for discussion during therapy rather than of criticism for preferring this material.

Much discussion in this country at the present time, inevitably brings up the question of the 'Moors murders' and the personality of Brady and Hindley. Analysis of their early life history shows that Brady had a typical background in that he was illegitimate, had a reputation for cruelty before he was 10 and 'always carried a flick-knife'.

Hindley was brought up by her grandmother where she could stay out late and truant frequently from school.

Much was made of the literature and photographs found among their possessions but there is no hard evidence that it actually influenced their behaviour. It was coincidental – as with my patients.

On the other hand, one must take note of the prevalence of violence in the mass media such as television. Wertham states that in one analysis, in one week, one station on American television showed 334 completed or attempted killings and that the total channels in one city showed in one week 7,887 acts of violence and 1,087 threats of violence. Saturation on this scale during childrens' viewing time must condition them to take life cheaply. Even in this country we have seen a man executed on the TV News and we have become accustomed to death and destruction and burning bodies in the same context as politics and sports and with no differentiation between them. There is certainly a case for the restriction of violence in this manner in a world where it is so much taken for granted.

This is more a case for common sense than for formal censorship however.

(*a*) Adults should be informed of the violence in our lives. This is one of the important factors in a book like *Last Exit*.
(*b*) Children should not be subject to saturation of violence as at present.
(*c*) Sadistic literature, and even sadistic film or theatre, if in correct context, can be informative and abreactive.

I personally would allow both so called pornographic and sadistic literature in prisons. I believe it would relieve and not provoke tension.

(*c*) DRUGS

The problem of drug taking, particularly hard drug taking has been with us in steadily increasing amount for the last 4 to 5 years. I have a Drug Dependence Treatment Unit at my hospital and we were one of the first to treat heroin dependent patients in any great numbers in hospital. I have therefore considerable experience of the problem.

There is no doubt at all in my mind that the emotional publication of 'drug stories' in certain newspapers has glamorised the problem and I have had a number of addicts under my care who kept scrap books or even pasted all the clippings concerning their friends on the wall. Publication in this way is to be deplored.

On the other hand, many people, members of parliament, social workers, ministers, etc. have to come to grips with this problem and, apart from learning 'the hard way' by working with addicts, they can gain great insight into their problems by reading some of the very sensitive and revealing books written about them or by them and this I would say was one of the accepted methods of communication.

(4) SUGGESTION FOR REFORM

(1) The present very confused situation with recourse to so many

Acts, etc. in order to obtain conviction; the variation in procedure, attitudes, and tolerance among individual magistrates and in different settings should be clarified.

(2) Emotionality should be removed from the situation by ceasing to use emotionally toned words such as 'indecent' and 'obscene'. I know that these words have been defined but it is very difficult to use them impartially.

(3) The freedom of the individual should be respected and I can see no reason to restrict the freedom of adults to do whatever they like in private so long as it does not involve others who may be influenced to their detriment. It is extremely difficult to define these limits as they cover such a wide field of activity.

smoking tobacco (associated in advertisements with sex).
drinking alcohol (associated in advertisements with manliness).
nudity.
reading or seeing what one wishes.

These are examples of activities in which the authorities have taken varying degrees of interest in an attempt to curtail them.

For the mature individual there would appear to be no rational reason for interference and indeed as we have seen, maturity cannot be reached without experience and education and it is this that censorship so often curtails in its own fear and ignorance.

A short bibliography to indicate the source of some of the material. Title and Author only.

(1) Burroughs	*Junkie*
(2) Burroughs	*The Naked Lunch*
(3) De Sade	*Justine*
(4) Durgnat	*Eros in the Cinema*
(5) Freeman	*The Undergrowth of Literature*
(6) Gebhard *et al.*	*Sex Offenders*
(7) Greenwald	*The Call Girl*
(8) Hughes	*The Fantastic Lodge*
(9) Hyde	*A History of Pornography*
(10) Kinsey	*Sexual Behaviour in the Human Male and Female*
(11) Keyes	*All Night Stand*

(12) Kronhauser	*Walter – My Secret Life*
(13) Leech and Jordan	*Drugs*
(14) Levy	*The Artist and the Nude*
(15) Marcus	*The Other Victorians*
(16) Masters and Johnson	*Human Sexual Response*
(17) Michaux	*Light Through Darkness*
(18) Miller	*Tropic of Cancer*
(19) Potter	*The Monster of the Moors*
(20) Sacher-Masoch	*Venus in Furs*
(21) Schur	*Narcotic Addiction*
(22) Storr	*Sexual Deviation*
(23) Straker	*Nudes*
(24) Trocchi	*Cain's Book*
(25) Ullerstam	*The Erotic Minorities*
(26) Walker	*Sex in the Movies*
(27) Wertham	*A Sign for Cain*
(28) Wolgang and Ferracuti	*The Subculture of Violence*
(29) Wolpe and Lazarus	*Behaviour Therapy Techniques*
(30) Young	*Eros Denied*

Appendix E.ii

Report received from Mr A. Gooch, LL.B.

Chief Clerk, Marlborough Street Magistrates' Court and a member of the London Magistrates' Clerks' Association

Issues of Indecency and Obscenity in the Magistrates' Courts

The Magistrates' Courts have no jurisdiction (within the scope of this enquiry) to deal with Common Law offences and therefore this note is only concerned with statutory offences which can be tried summarily.

Those which occur with any frequency in central London are reduced to three in number; the others being rarely invoked. These three are:

(1) Vagrancy Act, 1824, Section 4.
(2) Post Office Act, 1953, Section 11.
(3) Obscene Publications Act, 1959, Section 2.

(1) THE VAGRANCY ACT, 1824, SECTION 4
creates several offences

One is 'wilfully exposing to view in any street or public place or in the window or other part of any shop or other building situate in any street any obscene print, picture or other indecent exhibition'. Basically this is a street offence. In modern conditions the section will be most commonly invoked in the case of unusually revealing 'strip-club' or 'film-club' advertisements displayed either outside the premises or by the doorman to passers-by. The literary element is not normally involved. It did arise in one case where some paintings by Jim Dine were displayed in a gallery and several appeared to show the male characteristic organ (and little else) in one picture apparently in copulation with female genitals. There was evidence that the pictures were visible from the street, and evidence that they had caused offence: whether they were indecent was an issue for the Magistrate to decide, and having seen the pictures in evidence he decided that they were.

(2) POST OFFICE ACT, 1953, SECTION 11

'A person shall not send or attempt to send or procure to be sent a postal packet which encloses any indecent or obscene print painting photograph lithograph engraving film book card or written communication, or any indecent or obscene article whether similar to the above or not.'

The Post Office does not wish to be a carrier of indecent matter. In practice the contents of postal packets are only revealed when a complaint is made by the recipient of unsolicited and undesired material, or the post may originate in England and be opened by a foreign Post Office such as that of the U.S.A. The person who posted the offending material is then traced back and prosecuted.

A person who answers an advertisement in the hope of receiving obscene material in return commits an offence (even if the advertisement is fraudulent so that no such material would be posted). It is also an offence for the recipient of unwanted and unsolicited indecent material to post it back to the sender.

Here again the Magistrate is the judge of what is indecent or obscene. Those two words have been judicially defined as the bottom (or least offensive) and top (or most offensive) of a scale of prohibited matter. It is the article complained of which forms the evidence and the Magistrate's view alone determines whether or not the section applies to it.

(3) OBSCENE PUBLICATIONS ACT, 1959, SECTION 2

It is an offence to publish an obscene article or to have an obscene article for publication for gain (whether gain for oneself or another).

It is not an offence merely to have obscene material: the offender must either publish it or contemplate a publication for gain.

The operation of the section, the statutory definition in the Act of obscenity and the statutory defence of public good are well known.

This section is rarely applied in Magistrates' Courts to books for which quality is claimed, and these cases are in any event notorious. It is used most commonly for the seller of 'dirty books' for which no literary quality is ever claimed. (The price of such material is vastly in excess of its production costs. In turn some hopelessly innocent material may be marked up at an excessive price to catch the purchaser who takes cost to indicate content.)

Proceedings under Section 3 (search for and seizure of obscene articles) may now only be sought by the Director of Public Prosecutions or a constable.

At Marlborough Street I would put the number of relevant prosecutions annually at about:

Vagrancy Act	3–6
Post Office Act	3
Obscene Publications Act	12–20

THE JUDICIAL APPROACH

Magistrates are judges of fact and of law. Thus they have to come to a finding of fact on the evidence presented to them and apply the relevant law to it. They should direct themselves on the point to be decided as a Judge directs a Jury.

A Bench may receive evidence of the circumstances of publication, and even take outside help on the meaning of words, e.g. 'indecent', (by referring to a dictionary) but Magistrates are the final judges and the issue cannot be decided for them by the witnesses. Thus the Bench must pay due regard to the evidence offered, and should accept it if unchallenged, but they must resolve all the points in issue themselves. They, and not witnesses, must give a ruling as to what is the meaning of 'indecent' or 'obscene' and apply that definition to the work in the case. They will, of course, be governed by binding judicial definitions.

The evidence of a particular witness as to whether an article is indecent under the Vagrancy or Post Office Acts is inadmissable because his view is not relevant in the legal sense. The only opinion permitted is that of the Magistrates.

On the other hand the Obscene Publications Act 1959 allows evidence of opinion about the effect of the article to be given (but not to define 'obscene'). This is sometimes called expert evidence, but 'expert' does not mean a witness so accomplished that his view must prevail and rule the judgement of the Bench. An expert is a witness who, by reason of his experience, is allowed to draw a conclusion from given facts, where a conclusion is relevant to the issue for decision. The Bench must evaluate his evidence. A parallel example may be given from the offence of dangerous driving. Evidence of the fact of an accident may be given, and an expert may be allowed to draw a conclusion as to the state of a vehicle before the accident, but no witness may say that the driving was 'dangerous' because that is the issue for the Bench alone.

Thus Magistrates have also to decide if a particular work is obscene. The witnesses' evidence only goes to the issue of public good. As there is no common view of obscenity as a demonstrable state of fact to bind all Magistrates different results in different Courts on 'arguable' material are inevitable.

I have never heard any evidence being called to show that any depravity or corruption has in fact been induced by a work. It is always left for the Court to infer that consequence if the work itself appears to support it.

Finally I must add a note that any comments I have made represent a personal view, and certainly are not in any way the expressed opinions of the Magistrates of this Court.

Appendix E.iii
Summary of Statement to Arts Council Working Party, Answers to Questions etc.

from Mr James D. Halloran, B.Sc.(Econ.), Director, University of Leicester Centre for Mass Communication Research

(A) GENERAL

Current generalisations about the influence of mass media indicate that the media rarely work directly on people but operate indirectly, being affected by such factors as personality, predisposition, past experience, present affiliations and attitudes, and future anticipations. It is further suggested that the overall tendency is to reinforce what is already there rather than to create or put new things there – and that on the whole well formed attitudes and values are not likely to be changed by exposure to the media.

These statements are all right as far as they go, but they should be recognized for what they are – tentative generalisations stemming from research already carried out, most of it in the U.S.A. It is important to recognize the following qualifications:

(*a*) The intervening factors which are frequently seen as 'filtering' the message need not operate solely in one specific way, i.e. as a filter. They may work in the same direction as the message, perhaps giving it greater impact – or they may not be working at all.

(*b*) The mass media may have little impact where attitudes and values are well formed, but what of the areas – perhaps vital social areas – where this is not the case. A young person in a rapidly changing society where traditional social controls are no longer operative may be a case in point.

(*c*) Generalisations from research dealing with adults are not necessarily applicable to young people. Very little research has been carried out on the role of the media in the early stages of child development.

(*d*) Some of the models used to guide many research exercises – exercises which on the whole have shown the media to have little influence – have been so crude or inappropriate that they could hardly have been expected to show anything else. If we look for fundamental changes immediately after exposure we are unlikely to find them, but if we could develop our research instruments to capture the slow, gradual adjustments and accretions over time then we might find a different picture of change which in the long run might be quite substantial.

The mass media can and do influence values and behaviour. They are likely to have maximum impact when there is repetition, when emotions are brought into play, when needs or interests are being met, and where the person concerned has not been provided with an adequate set of standards or criteria against which to judge or assess the 'message'.

There are obviously groups and individuals in our society who are particularly vulnerable or susceptible to certain forms of appeal and to certain types of media fare. The maladjusted, the friendless, certain categories of delinquent, etc. have all been shown to use the media in certain distinctive ways, usually to feed the problem rather than to solve it, although it should be remembered that to establish a relationship between two factors, e.g. isolates and heavy media consumption, need not tell us anything about the direction of the relationship or whether the outcome is good or bad in social terms.

In a differentiated, stratified, pluralistic society, one way of defining the research problem is as an attempt to identify groups and individuals in terms of differential media usage. The main research question is not What do the media do to people? but How do certain people, with certain predispositions, backgrounds, attitudes, etc. use certain types of media in certain situations? What functions are performed by the media at various levels within society and what are the overall consequences of this functioning?

It also needs to be stressed that in the multi-valued society where people also occupy different roles and belong to different strata these factors influence more than reaction to the media. Issues and situations are perceived and analysed, problems diagnosed and solutions offered not 'objectively' but in terms of these positions. Except in one or two central areas there may be very little agreement on 'bad' effects and 'good' effects at the concrete behavioural level – even if these effects could be firmly established. We also have the problem of double or contrary effects (different people – different impact). In many ways one man's media meat may be another man's media poison. Obviously there are certain categories that need protection, and certain areas (e.g. portrayal of violence) where one must be extremely cautious. However, we must also be careful to avoid equating change with deterioration. What is regarded as a change for the better by some may be regarded as a disaster by others.

I presume that at centre this is what the censorship debate is about. It often takes the form of rival vested interests (economic, professional, moral, religious) stating their case on the alleged effect or lack of effect of a certain media product on an ill-defined, selectively perceived 'vital' value area.

Evidence linking specific media products to specific effects is rarely if ever produced. In a way this is not surprising for so little evidence is available, and in turn this is not surprising for the research effort in this area has been so meagre. Perhaps one would not expect the 'censors' to submit their 'censorious mythologies' to objective and rigorous research, but one would hope for a somewhat different approach from what may be termed the other side. Unfortunately there is little evidence that writers, artists, publishers, producers, etc. are anxious to submit their 'freedom mythologies' to social-scientific probes or examination. The debate on the effects of pornography didn't start yesterday. Yet what steps have been taken in this country by writers, publishers,

Government, Arts Council, etc. to promote the research which would provide the information which would make the debate a more informed and enlightened one, and would eventually lead to a deeper understanding of vital social issues and problems? In this, as in many other areas, we have surely got past the stage where we can make do with an exchange of prejudices. If we want the facts we must promote and support research. Those with commercial interests are certainly willing to do this in their field. The *annual* cost in this country of administrative and commercially oriented media research certainly exceeds £3 million – about sixty times more than the annual amount spent on *all forms* of media research, the type of which would go some way to answering the questions with which we are concerned. Perhaps we should question the values behind these investments.

It is not surprising when one realises that the media are so often singled out as scapegoats for society's ills that much of the research effort in this field has been concentrated on effect studies. However, it needs stressing that there is much more to research than this, and much more to the communication process than effects.

It is more or less inevitable that we have to wait a long time for research results, but we might have to wait longer than we need if we ask the wrong questions at the outset. It is tempting to attempt to devise research methods that can be applied in ways and in areas where there is a good chance that a neat cause and effect relationship will be produced. Unfortunately, this can often lead to 'the definitive about the irrelevant and the inconsequential'. It is not particularly useful to allow the socially relevant to be defined by methodological availability, and it is certainly unwise to suspend research activity in the absence of a 'perfect' method.

There are methods available now which, although by no means perfect, can certainly deepen our understanding of mass communication as a social process and of mass media as social institutions. This, after all, is basically what we seek to know. This implies, of course, that we should give attention to content, audience and the production process as well as to effects. It is absolutely essential to study the whole mass communication process within the wider social context, and this includes economic and political control and support factors as well as decision-making at all levels within the media industry. Our own research has shown us that it is important to study the producer (using this term in its widest sense) to ascertain how he sees his role, and to learn about his background, conditions of work, attitudes, values and intentions. It is the total process we need to study.

(B) MEDIA VIOLENCE AND AGGRESSION

There is no doubt that there is widespread public concern about the media portrayal of violence and aggression. The claim often made but never substantiated is that the reading about or viewing of violent incidents, etc. leads to an imitation of the violent behaviour or a general increase in aggressive behaviour. On the other hand, it is also claimed by some that media violence can have a beneficial influence producing a release of tension, a lowering of frustration, thus reducing the risk of violent behaviour.

Most of the research into the influence of media violence has been of an experimental nature carried out in laboratory situations, often to a test a cathartic-type hypothesis. The evidence from American studies offers little support for the catharsis argument. However, there is slight support from one or two Italian studies, and some Australian work suggests the possibility of a double effect. In general the evidence from these laboratory studies is usually taken as indicating that heavy exposure to media violence increases the possibility of violent behaviour in the post-exposure situation.

Again, it is necessary to put forward some qualifications. The main one concerns the limitation of this type of laboratory experiment and the danger in generalizing from such work to social situations in everyday life. This is not to say that the laboratory studies are a waste of time. On the contrary they can be most useful (assuming their limitations are recognized) when used together with other approaches (e.g. surveys, observations, depth interviews, etc.). An example of a comprehensive research strategy, calling for the interdisciplinary use of different methods, was outlined in the First Progress Report of the Television Research Committee.*

It should also be noted that most of the aforementioned experiments have attempted to assess only relatively short-term effects, mainly in terms of either limitation or increased aggressive drive. There are, of course, other ways of looking at the problem, particularly in the long run. One study indicates that heavy exposure to media (this includes reading material) violence and aggression leads to an 'ideology' which entails the acceptance of the legitimate use of force and aggression in one's self-interest, and a decrease in the willingness to oppose or resist violent behaviour in real-life situations. There is a suggestion from some Swedish work that long-term exposure to media violence is related to a tendency towards the use of violence in problem-solving. Psychiatric case studies from several sources have stressed the increased willingness to accept violence as well as the long-term desensitizing, brutalising effects which flow from regular exposure to 'violence as an everyday occurrence'.

In addition, our own work has shown that delinquents as distinct from non-delinquents are more oriented to media excitement and violence and that they are more inclined to blur their perceptions of reality and aggression. (What is aggressive is seen as real and what is real is seen as aggressive.) This apparent lack of discrimination is usually associated with high involvement in the programme or book. When this is taken together with the finding that impact or effect is influenced by involvement, then the importance of this finding becomes clear and the need for follow-up and further exploration essential.

Another of our studies has shown that it is important not to confine one's attention to the violence produces violence equation. This study showed violence producing regression and anxiety, and points to the need for much greater refinement in our definitions and conceptualisations. What is violence? How is it

* *Problems of Television Research,* First Progress Report of the Television Research Committee, Leicester University Press, 1966.

Other publications of the Television Research Committee are:

Working Paper No. 1, *The Effects of Mass Communication with Special Reference to Television,* Leicester University Press, 1964.

Working Paper No. 2, *Attitude Formation and Change,* Leicester University Press, 1967.

defined, both in terms of stimulus (media material) and response (attitude or behaviour)? How do different people perceive different forms of violence and aggression (we know there are differences in perception)? How important is the context? (Research has shown that legitimized and socially-approved as well as rewarded violence can have detrimental effects.) What are the other (non-violent) effects we ought to look for? Can the portrayal of violence have beneficial social effects (e.g. serving as a danger signal or as a catalyst)? These are the questions that we ought to ask, and they can be paralleled in other (non-violent) areas. It is true that at this stage in the work there are more questions than answers, but this is not necessarily a bad thing. A great deal of basic spadework and ground-clearing have been carried out and at least we are now in the fortunate position of knowing what questions to ask. This is the essential starting point. We also have the methods, although methodological sophistication will avail us nothing if we don't ask the right questions in the first place. The main thing holding us back today is quite simply that not enough research is being carried out. If we want answers to our questions, we must be prepared to invest more in the research effort.

Appendix E.iv
Law of Obscenity by Professor R. M. Jackson, J.P., LL.D., F.B.A.

Downing Professor of the Laws of England in the University of Cambridge

The essence of 'an article' being held to be obscene is that its effect is such as to tend 'to deprave and corrupt persons who are likely, having regard to all the relevant circumstances, to read, see or hear the matter contained or embodied in it'. It is not necessary in a prosecution to produce any evidence to show that the article would have such a tendency. The position as regards the effect of obscene publications is very different from that of drugs; we *know* the effects that some drugs produce, and this can be proved by evidence of persons who deal with drug addicts. The supposed depravity and corruption produced by obscene articles is a matter of conjecture; no hard evidence can be put forward, for nobody can demonstrate that anybody has ever been depraved or corrupted by a particular obscene article. A decision that an article would have such a tendency is based entirely upon opinion unsupported by verified facts. The Lord Chief Justice has used words which suggest that expert evidence can show the effect of a picture on children.* Magistrates had refused to hear the evidence of a child psychiatrist about the effect on children because of an old common law rule that evidence is not admissible when it goes to the very issue that the court has to determine. The Lord Chief Justice pointed out that the question whether a particular article tended to deprave and corrupt is (on summary trial) entirely for the justices to determine, but that it is entirely proper for an expert in child psychiatry to say what in his view would be the effect on children of certain kinds of picture and to put before him particular pictures involved in the case and ask his opinion on them. The Lord Chief Justice pointed out that it is these days acceptable to ask psychiatrists for opinions on a defendant's diminished responsibility, the effect of a particular thing on the body, and other matters that may be in issue. But surely there is a profound difference between a psychiatrist's opinion that particular pictures are likely to be harmful to children and an opinion on the mental state of a particular patient or the toxicity of a particular substance: evidence of an individual's mental state or of toxicity of a substance rests on observed facts (unless the witness is a charlatan).

Is it possible to conduct any experiment or enquiry that would produce factual evidence as to whether persons are depraved or corrupted by reading, seeing or hearing particular kinds of material? It would seem quite impossible to do so. We are deluged with pictures and writing, with sound radio and television, abounding with scenes of violence, stress on sex and assertion of paramount importance of various forms of personal attributes, possessions, behaviour and so on. We know that some of the deluge comes from people with genuine convictions as to what is

* *D.P.P.* v. *A. & B.C. Chewing Gum Ltd* (1967) 2 All E.R. 504.

right or true or desirable, much comes from a desire to make money by selling services or products and undoubtedly one kind of trade is concerned to meet (and increase) the demand for pornography. Our society has many people whose minds and emotions are warped and whose bodies reflect many woes, and it is possible that the state of some of them has been affected by pornography, but the difficulty of proof is formidable. Suppose we made a survey of all the pictures, writing, radio and television dealing with sex and violence that has been produced for public consumption, what proportion of it could, on current tests, be thought to be obscene? I think it would be a minute proportion. If then we could somehow establish that a particular person had been depraved and corrupted by what he had seen, read and heard about sex or violence, we should still have to show that his depravity and corruption was due to the small proportion of pornography rather than to the deluge of non-pornographical sex and violence to which he has been subjected.

Is there then any good reason for continuing to have criminal prohibition of obscene publications? The answer must depend on our attitude to the criminal law. If we take the view that the criminal law should not prohibit and penalise any conduct unless such conduct can be shown to have harmful effects, then we should get rid of the present offences. But if we look at the criminal law as it has been over the years we have to recognise that the purpose of some offences is to support and maintain various conceptions of acceptable conduct. A widespread change of public opinion may result in prosecutions ceasing to be brought, as with the crime of blasphemy. Any substantial change of the criminal law has to be made by Act of Parliament, and where there is widespread belief in the wrongfulness of certain behaviour it may be very difficult to get legislation. The crime of suicide (prosecuted of course as an attempt to commit suicide) lingered on for many years after the case for its abolition had been established, the law being altered by the Suicide Act 1961. Homosexual acts between consenting adult males in private were criminal until the Sexual Offences Act 1967, there being strong opposition to the Bill resting largely on unsubstantiated assertions of the harmful effects of such conduct. An important argument in favour of that legislation was that the criminal sanction against male homosexual acts had some positively bad effects. Many of the safest and most lucrative blackmailing practices depended on male homosexual acts being criminal thus making it unlikely that the victim would squeal.

If my argument is accepted that there is no hard evidence of anyone being depraved and corrupted by obscenity, the logical conclusion is that Parliament should remove obscenity from the criminal calendar, but is it realistic to press for that solution? I think not. At present there is a very considerable body of opinion that regards at least the cruder kind of obscenity as being socially harmful and properly a matter for criminal prohibition. When horror comics were prohibited by the Children and Young Persons (Harmful Publications) Act 1953 there was general agreement that such publications are harmful to the young, and the same kind of argument is applied to obscene material. On 3 February 1969 a judge at Leeds Assizes sentenced a man to two years' imprisonment for possessing for publication for gain copies of volumes one and two of *My Secret Life* by Walter, and on two similar charges concerning two other works.* Even if we make full allowance for judicial institutions being half a century or so out of step with current society, we can hardly regard the present as a propitious time for thorough-going rational reform. The wisest course is to postpone the major challenge and see what we can do about the present legal terrors.

If we take a broad look at the whole field of what are described as obscene publications, a striking feature is the large scale of the market for hard core pornography. Nobody knows the output of that material but we can get some idea from figures that are given from time to time in Parliament as to seizures by the Customs and by other authorities. Thus we learn that between 1961 and 1963 the Customs and the police seized 1,863,000 obscene novels which had been imported into Britain, the figures for the year 1964 being over 400,000 obscene novels and 597,000 obscene magazines. The Attorney General was naturally less explicit over home-produced pornography though he pointed out that in one recent seizure the police had seized 8 tons of such material.† The market was apparently unaffected because in 1965 seizure of

* *The Times,* 4 February, 1969.

† The Attorney-General in debate on the adjournment, 3 July, 1965.

imports amounted to 180,808 books and 1,760,139 magazines. The Attorney was asked about the size of staff employed to arrive at the conclusion that this quantity of material should be designated pornographical and the Attorney replied: 'It does not need a great staff: this stuff is filthy trash which no one has any difficulty in identifying.'*

This reply of the Attorney General is really crucial to the problem. There is in reality no difficulty at all in recognising what is commonly called 'hard core pornography' when one sees it. These seizures are not contested in court for the very good reason that no defence is possible. The real trouble is to put into legislation an intelligible definition that will distinguish between this hard core stuff and what is said to be the work of serious writers and artists.

As a starting point we can ask whether the present basic definition in terms of tendency to deprave and corrupt should not be replaced. My inclination is to leave it unaltered: it is true that it is thoroughly misleading and somewhat absurd, but it has been current since the decision in Hicklin† in 1868 and I regard it as having become part of English legal language. It is akin to 'malice aforethought' which in ordinary parlance does not connote malice or thought at any particular period of time. The law is full of such expressions and I see no advantage in getting rid of them unless one can put in their place something that is better. That was the view of the Select Committee on Obscene Publications, who added: 'We have indeed been offered only one other definition, which we do not consider to be an improvement'.‡ If the definition is left as it stands at present what we want is a method of protecting serious work against those who are too zealous in prosecuting. Most people thought that such protection would be given by the new provisions in s.4 of the Obscene Publications Act 1959, that is the defence of public good§ and the admissibility of the opinion of experts. That provision has resulted in a conception of balancing the 'good'

* The Attorney-General replying to a Question.

† R. v. *Hicklin* (1868) 3 Q.B. 360.

‡ Para. 13 of their Report (1958).

§ ('... if it is proved that publication of the article in question is justified as being for the public good on the ground that it is in the interests of science, literature, art or learning, or of other objects of general concern.')

attributes against the 'bad'. In fact of course we do not know whether the balancing process has actually taken place or not: for example in the *Lady Chatterley* case we do not know whether the jury decided among themselves that the novel is not obscene or whether they decided that it is obscene, but that there is sufficient public good to justify the publication. The point is that a jury has to be directed on the lines that if they find the material is not obscene that finishes the matter, but if they find that it is obscene they must go on to decide whether there is any public good and if so whether there is enough public good to justify publication. This I think gives us the real weakness of the present position. The matter that ought to be decisive is whether there is substantial evidence of value for science, literature, art or learning or other objects of general concern. The Act, in section 4, requires the justification to be 'proved', which means that strong and persuasive evidence in favour of a literary or artistic production can be overborne by a greater weight of evidence against it. We must, I suppose, recognise that concepts of what is needed or desirable or permissible in the arts often results in disapproval by the prevailing orthodoxy, but disapproval does not put a prohibition on work that is disliked; raise a question of obscenity, and then disapproval can secure suppression and punishment.

To get a formulation based on the principle that substantial evidence of value is a good defence, it is worth considering a test of obscenity adopted in the United States Supreme Court in 1966:* 'It must be established that (*a*) the dominant theme of the material taken as a whole appeals to a prurient interest in sex; (*b*) the material is patently offensive because it affronts contemporary community standards relating to the description or representation of sexual matters; and (*c*) the material is utterly without redeeming social value.' The first two requirements seem as open to objection as our own test of tendency to deprave and corrupt, but the last requirement suggests a way out of our difficulty. If we have, say, a novel that a jury is quite likely to regard as obscene and the defence call expert evidence of its literary merit, the judge would have to direct the jury that they could not find a verdict of guilty unless it is 'utterly without redeeming social value'. It might

* *Memoirs* v. *Massachusetts* 383 U.S. 413.

make a good deal of difference whether this is to be regarded as a defence or as part of the definition of obscenity. If the former it would mean that if the jury found the work to be obscene it would be their duty to convict unless the defence shows that there is some redeeming social value. If it were to be the latter the jury would have to be directed that they could not convict unless they found that the work is obscene and that it is utterly without redeeming social value. I should very much prefer to see the latter formulation.

Suppose we did get the law altered in the way I have suggested, can we be sure that that would give adequate protection to authors and publishers? I would not like to be too sure about that because I think we have two things that stand in the way. The first is that virtually everyone who reads books or looks at pictures feels that he is a competent judge of their merits. Hence, when magistrates or jurymen read or see the work that is being attacked, they are apt to come to a conclusion about its obscenity or otherwise. The second is that there is a fairly wide distrust of expert witnesses; that distrust has I think been fanned by exaggerated statements made by some witnesses in some obscenity trials and by some psychologists and psychiatrists in other trials. It is always difficult to get a person to alter his view when he has already made up his mind and hence I think we have to accept that there is always a possibility of magistrate or juror coming to a firm decision in his own mind and then paying virtually no attention to the evidence that he subsequently hears. I see no way round that. The most we can hope for is to devise tests and procedures that may be expected to work better than the present ones but not to look for perfection.

I have no knowledge of the extent to which other statutes are used in cases of alleged obscenity, i.e.:
The Vagrancy Act 1824 section 4;
The Town Police Clauses Act 1847, section 28;
The Indecent Advertisements Act 1889, sections 3 and 4;
The Post Office Act 1953, section 11;
The Children and Young Persons Harmful Publications Act 1955 and Customs Consolidation Act 1876.

Local by-laws are used for dealing with minor matters of indecent behaviour in public but I do not think they can be used to suppress writing, pictures and so on. Vagrancy is one of the statutes that is likely to be reviewed before long.

The common law position is most unsatisfactory. It did appear that the practice of charging common law misdemeanours was being restricted, but in two respects events of the last few years have been disquieting. The offence of conspiracy can cover the agreement of two or more people to do anything of which the judges strongly disapprove. It may also be used to boost up minor offences so that people who protest by sitting down in a street may be prosecuted for a conspiracy if it can be shown that they agreed to commit that particular kind of obstruction of the highway. The result is that it is an indictable offence with no legal limit to the length of imprisonment, or to the amount of fine that may be imposed. The case of R. v. *Clayton and Halsey** shows that a charge of conspiracy to commit an offence under the Obscene Publications Act can by-pass the safeguards contained in the 1959 Act because the charge is conspiracy and not obscenity. The Law Commission have the matter of common law offences under consideration.

The other alarming case is, of course, that of the *Ladies Directory*.† A charge that was successful, namely conspiracy to corrupt public morals, shows the way in which a charge of conspiracy may be used. The worst feature of the case was, however, the vigorous assertion by Lord Simonds that the court is *custos morum* of the people, for which of course there is judicial authority from the 17th century onwards. It is, however, a somewhat astonishing doctrine these days to say that in the last resort the way we can behave, the things we can read, look at, hear and presumably enjoy, are subject to Big Brother wigged and gowned on the judicial bench. The decision has been much criticised by lawyers‡ and inasmuch as it all rests on common law misdemeanour it falls under the review that the Law Commission is undertaking.

It is now accepted that the criminal law is to be codified and

* (1962) 3 W.L.R. 815.

† *Shaw* v. *D.P.P.* (1962) A.C. 220.

‡ Strong comment was made by Professor Seaborne Davies, 6 Journal Society of Public Teachers of Law, 104.

among many of the problems that that raises is whether when the Code is completed and becomes law there should be in it a provision that all offences must be prosecuted under sections of the Code or under other legislation. Such a rule is to be found in criminal Codes within the Commonwealth, and that of course would get rid of the nonsense of the *Ladies Directory* case. It will, however, be necessary to continue having an offence of conspiracy though somehow or other it should be far more limited than it is at present.

Appendix E.v
Statement made by Mr Thomas Joy, F.R.S.A.

Past-President of the Booksellers Association of Great Britain and Ireland and a member of the Working Party

An additional argument against the existing Acts representing what seems to be a legitimate grievance of booksellers is that it is obviously absurd for a bookseller to be prosecuted under any of the Acts when he cannot possibly read all the books. Even if he could, he is no judge of literature in all fields and, in any case, he has no right to act as a censor. The publisher is in a very different position and as long as a bookseller has bought his stock from a reputable British publisher, he should be in the clear. One might as well confiscate a chemist's stock, or prosecute him, because someone says he suffered ill effects from a particular drug (after all, aspirin is poison).

The law must be changed so that a bookseller is regarded as being a member of a fine profession and not as a purveyor of pornography, an image which, I am afraid, he is rapidly gaining.

Appendix E.vi
Statement from Miss Margaret Miles, B.A.

Headmistress of a London Girls' Comprehensive School

I find it difficult to comment on the headings that you have given me as I do not know in practice what is the actual effect of these various pieces of legislation.

With regard to No. 3,* however, one can have an impression but this can hardly be said to be 'solid evidence'. I would have thought that literature and the arts were not directly responsible for the attitudes of young people toward sex, violence, drugs, but literature and the arts themselves tend to reflect the values of society and on the whole people get what they are looking for. I find it difficult to believe that people would read *Lady Chatterley's Lover* or *Fanny Hill* and get depraved thereby. Many people who would be looking for that kind of stimulus from the books would probably fail to get it because they would be surprised by the amount of solid and rather boring reading they would have to do. This, I think, applies to a good many novels which some people might feel not suitable for a school library. I have always felt myself that if the work is of value it should be in the library and people will read it and respond to it at different levels.

Current literature and film in which swearing, drugs, promiscuity, etc. are taken for granted and which depict contemporary and recognisable people probably do suggest habits which can easily be passed on to others, but here again do they not reflect rather more than they guide society? Film and TV presumably have a much wider impact than literature, but the banning of *Lady Chatterley, Fanny Hill* and *Last Exit* gave a great boost to the sale of the books and therefore presumably extended their influence. What we just do not know is whether this influence was corrupting or depraving.

I do not know what to suggest in the way of reform in answer to question 4† because, as I say, there is no evidence of how much

* 3. 'What solid evidence there is relating to the effect of literature and the arts on behaviour in the fields of sex, violence and drugs and the extent, if any, to which people can be said to be depraved and corrupted by literature and the arts.'

† 4. 'Suggestions for reform.'

society is affected by arts and literature. Art and literature are not a sort of external mechanism for changing society for better or for worse.

Appendix E.vii
Statement from The National Union of Students

The National Union of Students is really not concerned with the Obscene Publications Act – and the other Acts – except in respect of the magazines or publications of students' unions in most colleges. Even here the crossing of the threshold into the area of obscenity is not considerable, but, nevertheless, the editors and publishers of these magazines would be well advised to understand, at least in broad terms, what are the provisions of the Obscene Publications Acts.

Student newspapers are now an important expression of student opinion within a college community. Student publications and the student press are a valuable aid in establishing and maintaining an atmosphere of free and responsible discussion and of intellectual exploration on the campus. They are a means of bringing student concerns to the attention of the institutional authorities and of formulating student opinion on various issues on the campus and in the campus at large.

A student press should be free of censorship and advance approval of copy, and its editors and managers should be free to develop their own editorial policies and news coverage.

The integrity and responsibility of student publications should be encouraged by arrangements which permit financial autonomy or ideally, complete financial independence.

We advise editors and managers of student publications to subscribe to canons of responsible journalism.

Appendix E.viii
Statement from Dr Anthony Storr, M.R.C.P., D.P.M,

a practising psychiatrist

I am unable to comment on the first two matters* to which you refer since I have no experience of the working of the Obscene Publications Acts in practice, nor do I know how much other Acts are used to censor or restrict literature. I may, however, be permitted to make some comment on the third item:† so far as I know, there is very little solid evidence relating to the effect of literature and the arts on behaviour in the fields of sex, violence and drugs, though there is a lot of uninformed comment and guesswork. So far as I have been able to discover from the literature, the general opinion is that the portrayal of violence, for instance, on the cinema or television only has an effect on people who are on the point of committing a violent act anyway. That is, there may be some reason to suppose that if a person is feeling very tense, angry and violent within himself, that seeing a programme encouraging violence which makes him think that violence is permissible might tip him over into acting his impulse out. The same might be true of sexual feelings. However, I think it must be borne in mind that if one were to attempt to censor television or the cinema or literature on the grounds that they might possibly tip people over into acting out sexual or violent impulses, one would have to impose so extensive a censorship that the whole matter would become ridiculous. It would be rather like censoring the Bible on the grounds that erotic passages in the Bible might excite a few people sexually. It is, however, arguable that an exclusive diet of, for instance, violence on television may have long term effects which we do not as yet know about, and this subject is under active investigation in the

* (1) The working of the Obscene Publications Acts in practice.
(2) The effect to which in practice other Acts are used to censor or restrict literature and the arts.

† 'What solid evidence there is relating to the effect of literature and the arts on behaviour in the fields of sex, violence and drugs and the extent, if any, to which people can be said to be depraved and corrupted by literature and the arts'.

United States. One of the principle investigators is Professor Leonard Berkowitz of the University of Wisconsin who will in fact be coming to this country to conduct a conference on violence towards the end of August.

As regards the extent to which people can be said to be depraved or corrupted by literature, the answer to this question of course depends on your definition of being depraved or corrupted. When people use these terms they are very often referring to the idea that persons could, by reading literature for instance, be encouraged to engage in sexual perversions which they have never thought of. In my view, disturbances of sexuality of this kind have their origin in early childhood and are the result of the family environment to which the individual was exposed during his first five or six years. It is therefore highly unlikely that a book will have the effect of making somebody perverse who is not so already. My own view is that people who are afflicted with sexual perversions go out and find the literature which fits in with their own particular predilection. In other words, literature is secondary to the presence of perversion and does not induce or cause it.

I have no information about the effect of literature and the arts on the taking of drugs. I am quite prepared to believe that since drug-taking is fashionable at the moment this may have been encouraged to some extent by literature, but here again, research is gradually disclosing that those people who become addicted to drugs are people of a particular personality and that while it is true that if they had never been exposed to drug-taking they would not have become addicts, it is also true to say that the principal fault lies in the person rather than in the drug. I should certainly deplore the use of literature to encourage heroin-taking, for instance, but even if there were such literature I should require a great deal of convincing that it played a major part in causing addiction, though it might certainly play a minor contributory part.

Appendix E.ix
MEMORANDUM
(from Mr Jean Straker, Academy of Visual Art, London W.1)

In submitting this memorandum it is necessary for me to make some preliminary remarks:

(1) I speak from a position of total involvement in the obscenity laws, having been prosecuted firstly under the 1959 Act, and then under the combined 1959–64 Acts, as well as the Post Office Act.

In all these cases I have defended myself in the courts and have paid over £500 in fines and have lost over 1,400 original negatives of considerable artistic and scientific value.

(2) Art is a vehicle of communication and education, not merely a form of entertainment or escape. The talent brought by an artist in observing, recording and communicating facts and ideas is as important to the objective record of man as it is to his subjective perception. The laws which suppress information and expression in the field covered by the terms 'obscene' and 'indecent' are as much concerned with knowledge and scientific enquiry as they are with artistic creative innovation.

It is difficult at this level to separate art and science and I accordingly take the term 'art' to include that part of science which is concerned with human observation, notation and inference. I use the term 'cross-cultural' in this way professionally to describe my own work in the portrayal of the female nude in photographic art; in this definition I have been for many years a forerunner and advocate of inter-disciplinary concepts of study which are now being tried in many universities and para-university institutions. This is to say that any consideration of art potential in our time must take into account the factual, educational and disciplinary values of created work as well as the formal, artistic values. No creativity can now be treated as a subject in isolation: its formal abstraction from the society which has given it birth is inseparable from its socio-psychological involvement with and influence upon the organic development of that society.

(3) The argument that I shall present for the purpose of assisting the working party in its deliberations will be directed to and consistent with the Freedom of Vision proposal which are defined in a draft for a Freedom of Communications Bill* to abolish the terms 'obscene' and 'indecent' as definitions of crimes.

In that almost all I have to say has been said before, I will not burden the working party with the vast amount of documentary evidence relating to cases in which I have been involved, with the provision that I will provide any further information that may be sought on any matter mentioned.

THE WORKING OF THE OBSCENE PUBLICATIONS ACTS IN PRACTICE

When Charles Skilton, in 1957, made a selection of photographs from my Femina collection for publication as the book *Nudes of Jean Straker* he chose studies which showed no pubic hair, or, at the most, a tiny uncertain wisp which might be interpreted as a nondescript shadow.

At that time the Select Committee on the Obscene Publications Bill was taking evidence. In the context of a memorandum to the Committee, the Commissioner of Police for the Metropolis said:

> 'The courts usually adopt the view that a photograph of a male or female showing pubic hairs is obscene.' – (Minutes of Evidence, 122 HMSO, 20.3.58, p. 73.)

I wrote in the preface to the book at the time:

> 'To many good and otherwise civilised people the honest representation of the unblemished nude suggests wickedness and obscenity, in spite of her constant, noble and revered position in the cultured minds of men and the art galleries of the world.
>
> 'It is right that society shall protect itself against a degrading exploitation of the baser instincts; but it is equally important that its intellect shall remain unshackled and free to explore with probity the vast territory of man's vision.'

The words were ambiguous and evasive. You could not write openly about pubic hair then without censure; you can now.

* Superseded by the Obscene Publications (Amendment) Bill presented to the House of Commons by Mr William Hamling, M.P., on 25 March, 1969.

We published a photograph in the book of a Chinese-Malay girl, Shazie Laine, showing her hairless pubis with clear labial detail. This put paid to a current servicemen's slanderous joke about the anatomical orientation of an Oriental vulva, and succeeded in getting the book banned in Australia. It was also banned in Ireland, but we escaped prosecution in England, although we were told by Foyles that the Board of Trade had referred it to the Director of Public Prosecutions.

At that time the Home Secretary had said in a memorandum to the Select Committee, (Minutes of Evidence, p. 1) that his functions were domestic and international.

I quote:

'The Home Secretary deals in Parliament with legislative proposals, but not with questions of the application of the law in particular cases. The Home Office maintain records of proceedings in criminal courts in England, Wales and Scotland and distribute to the authorities concerned information which they receive about traffic in obscene works.'

And:

'Under an international convention for the suppression of and traffic in obscene publications of September 12th 1923 (ratified by the United Kingdom on December 11th 1925) Treaty Series No. 1 1926 (Cmd 2575) Her Majesty's Government agreed to take all measures to discover, prosecute and punish any person committing the offence of distributing by way of trade any obscene thing (the definition of obscenity is left to the law of each of the high contracting parties to formulate). Under Article 6 each Contracting Party undertook to inform the appropriate contracting party of any obscene object discovered in violation of the Convention in the territory of the former party which is believed to have come from or been produced in the latter's territory.'

In 1958 the Italian police referred a copy of a study of Pinky Russell, which I had called 'Sun Worship' to the British authorities, with the result that I was visited by two detectives from The Obscene Publications Department.

The picture is a simple shot of a girl leaning against a wall, with the shape of her absent bikini patterned white on her tanned body, her pubic hair where it ought to be, applying skin oil.

I was told by the detectives that it was an offence to show 'private parts' and that I had better stick to bottoms. They were very polite, asked to see more of my work, and they took about 100 prints away. A few days later they came back and said that Maurice Crump liked my work and wanted to keep it and could they have another set of prints for their own reference purposes. They gave me a form to sign saying that I agreed to the Receiver for the Metropolitan Police keeping the prints. I had signed my first (and only) disclaimer.

The disclaimer is an administrative device used by the police to enable them to succeed in an investigation without having to institute legal proceedings. In this way they are able to seize goods without difficulty or independent control, and so purport to uphold the letter of the law, while, at the same time leaving the co-operative purveyor in a position in which he can restock and carry on trading in an under-the-counter kind of way. It is a quiet, semi-secret rough justice which has neither public hearing nor accountability; it puts individual policemen in a position of 'easy trading' and justifies the charging of high prices by those who allege they are selling articles 'at risk'.

When this same picture of Pinky Russell was printed some ten years later in the 1967 Trinity term issue of 'Oxymoron', the Oxford City Police referred the publication to the Director of Public Prosecutions; at the same time, 11 May, 1967, detectives from the Obscene Publications Department, under warrant, seized eleven copies of this study, and other prints and negatives, from my studio premises.

A week later the photographs of Pinky Russell were returned to me and at the same time the Oxford City Police told the editor of 'Oxymoron' that there would be no prosecution in respect of their publication.

The context in which the photograph was published relates to the operation of the Obscene Publications Acts.

It is necessary to note that as the then editor of 'Oxymoron', Peter Adamson, had obtained proctorial consent prior to the publication of the photograph, to prosecute the magazine could have meant a challenge to Oxford University autonomy; but the decision did mean that there was a publication which did not attract prosecution some ten years after I had been told that such publication was illegal.

It is relevant here to record that during the hearing of the last case to be brought against me at the magistrates' court, and also subsequently at London Sessions during the hearing of the appeal, remarks were made which reflect a changing official attitude in these courts to the publication of photographs which show pubic hair.

At Marlborough Street magistrates' court on 24 October, 1967, the magistrate, John Aubrey-Fletcher said:

> 'I have looked at Mr Straker's photographs and there is not the slightest doubt that a great deal of them have extremely artistic value and cannot be regarded as indecent or obscene at all.
>
> 'I am going to take the view which may be more advanced than courts above have taken: I don't believe or hold that the display of pubic hair is in itself either indecent or obscene.'

And at Inner London Sessions, on Appeal, Reginald Seaton said:

> 'Well now, in this case let me preface my remarks by saying this: there is nothing wrong in picturing the female body; indeed many artists have done it in times gone by and still do it today, and lots of admirable paintings emerge. As the appellant has said, at one time it was regarded as becoming indecent when pubic hair appeared in pictures; but times change and I think today that this is not the case.'

It is necessary to note that these remarks were made in the course of judgements which went against me, so one must take it that my pictures were condemned for reasons other than the fact that they showed pubic hair.

Yet the remarks stand as direct contradictions of earlier and higher court decisions, and in the face of the usual opinion of the courts defined in the Commissioner of Police's report to the Select Committee.

It also means that prints and negatives seized before the change of attitude (including many of my negatives and prints) remain in official hands although they would not be considered indecent or obscene by the courts now.

In John Aubrey-Fletcher's judgment the terms 'obscene' and

'indecent' were both used; in Reginald Seaton's case the term 'indecent' was used alone.

According to the Lord Chief Justice (see Freedom of Vision report 'Censorship in the Arts', page 20, Richard DuCann) the terms 'indecent' and 'obscene' are defined as follows:

> 'There is a recognised standard of propriety: indecency is at the lower end of the scale in infringing that standard and obscenity is at the top end of the scale.'

It is necessary to note that the word 'obscene', used in the Obscene Publications Acts, has a definition, a test and a defence. No such qualifications are attached to the word 'indecent'. The Lord Chief Justice further defines a difference between the words 'obscene' and 'indecent' in the following words (CCA, 16.2.65, *D.P.P.* v. *Straker* – 'Censorship in the Arts', p. 65):

> 'It is an attractive point put by Mr Straker . . . that just as obscenity must be tested by the effect on the people to whom it may be published, so must questions of indecency relate to the people to whom they are published. Mr Straker prides himself on being very careful in his distribution, as he puts it, in only sending photographs to people who, he is quite satisfied, will not find them indecent. It is, as I said, an attractive way of saying it, but unfortunately the Post Office Act of 1953 does not so provide.'

There are two points here which should be observed. The first is that the Post Office Act uses both words 'obscene' and 'indecent'. In the action brought against me the word 'indecent' was used, thereby blocking any possible defence which might be mounted if the word 'obscene' were used.

But the second point is even more pertinent to the judgments given in the lower courts, which appear to be based on objective evaluation of the picture content. It makes the point that obscenity must be tested by the effect on the people seeing the matter published.

That is to say, there is no obscenity *per se* in law. My argument on this issue is contained in paragraphs 77–99 of my main affidavit, attached to the notice of motion in regard to Leo Gradwell's order of 9 April, 1962.

This argument is confirmed by Roy Jenkins in his letter to William Hamling dated 20 November, 1967 (printed with my talk to the Manchester Union Debating Society, dated 24 November, 1967).

Roy Jenkins says:

'It was for this reason that the definition of obscenity was so drawn as to take account of the people or audience to which a publication was addressed; what might be obscene if directed to – say – the general public might well not be so if directed to serious students.'

My detailed examination of this letter in relation to the Obscene Publications Acts is contained in the Manchester text.

It will be seen that the making of any objective decision on 'obscenity' ('The courts take the view that pubic hair is – or is not – obscene') is incompatible with a test on the people to whom the article is published, as required by section 1 of the 1959 Act.

My experiences in the courts under the 1959 Obscene Publications Act, and subsequently under the 1959 Act as amended by the 1964 Act, are given in my talk at the University of Leicester on 13 February, 1969.

You will see from the examination of the facts of my experiences, and from my arguments, that I have found the obscenity and indecency laws oppressive in the extreme – and in a way which Parliament did not intend.

In the House of Commons on 3 June 1964 (Parliamentary Debates, Vol. 695, 113, col. 1209) The Solicitor General said:

'The reason for this Bill is to strike at and to hit what I might call the Soho bookshop and the importers of prurient pornography.'

It does not need me to show the members of this working party that the powers which were given to the police failed to prevent the multiplication of Soho bookshops and failed to stop the importation of 'prurient pornography'.

Furthermore, as the Danish Government has now unilaterally denounced the 1923 Geneva Convention no action by the British authorities can now be used to suppress the production of any obscene matter, however judged, in Denmark.

The position is thus ridiculous, for it now means that the United Kingdom is bound by a treaty obligation which makes it impossible for an English photographer to produce work which may be legally published in an overseas country, because some magistrate here or in another country may consider it to be obscene. But the position is even more foolish than this, for anyone can now go into a British Post Office and obtain a money order payable in Denmark for the purchase of whatever he wants – while United Kingdom photographers are unable to compete by supplying a home-produced product. I have proof of the delivery in England, after 'Customs and Currency' examination, of a Danish magazine listing every type of 'sex pornography'.

Of course, the matter is not only an economic one; it is an educational and psychological issue also, for the legal restraints make it impossible for a photographer such as I am to meet an entirely bona fide demand for pictures for psychiatric use in hospitals and research use in universities. Many of the 1,400 negatives now held by the authorities were produced for such purposes.

My negatives are all large negatives, size 10″ × 8″, produced in my studio with great care, technical skill and artistic and scientific purpose.

Dr Peter Daws, from the Department of Psychology at the University of Leeds, gave evidence for me before the Marlborough Street magistrate on 7 January, 1966. During the course of this evidence he said:

> 'The problem of sexual research? And the problem of what other countries do have institutionalised protected research institutes? I have only been able to find one in Tokyo and one in Bloomington, Indiana, and one in Vienna. As a result of these recognised and protected institutions research involving these things does take place more widely than it does here. Certainly one of my feelings is that the great pity is that nothing like this has been started in this country and that if anything like this is to be started at all it must be done by private enterprise, perhaps in the face of a certain amount of public opposition. I have satisfied myself that Mr Straker is genuinely interested in what the court might call pornographic and what he calls gynaecographic studies for research activities and he exercises very considerable responsibility in the determination of the membership of that department.'

One would take it from section 4 of the 1959 Act – and from the interpretation placed upon that section by Roy Jenkins, when

Home Secretary, in his letter to William Hamling – that this type of evidence and opinion would be sufficient to block a judgment of obscenity.

But it is my experience of the workings of the Acts in the courts that section 4 defences are ignored and that decisions continue to be made on the basis of the magistrate's own opinion of the picture content.

What Reginald Seaton, Chairman of Inner London Quarter Sessions said in the last appeal which I made in the course of his Judgment (15 February, 1968) was:

> 'It is quite apparent and we are unanimous in forming the view that if young people got those pictures they did corrupt and deprave and therefore they are obscene, they are grossly obscene; and what the appellant is doing in our view is that he is covering up the sales of dirty pictures in a jargon of science which they do not merit.
>
> 'The sooner this business is stopped the better because, if you go on Mr Straker, you will find yourself going to prison for this and so you had better stop.'

It is necessary for me to say here that membership of my Academy and the Department of Gynaecographic Studies is limited to adults over 21, and that any 'scientific jargon' would be applied by the university research departments – the psychologists, the psychiatrists, the biologists, the anthropologists, etc. – who would use their own terms in the application and analysis of my photographs.

I would say, therefore, that the intended liberality of the 1959 Act has not been extended to serious writers, artists and photographers and that the intellectual arguments in relation to creativity and research are beyond the understanding of many of the magistrates who have to interpret the law. In fact, in failing to take into account the defence provision of section 4 of the 1959 Act, they have eviscerated that Act of its intended liberality.

And at the same time, it does not need me to tell the members of your working party that the intention of the laws to stop the trade in imported 'prurient pornography' has been wholly ineffective.

THE EFFECT TO WHICH IN PRACTICE OTHER ACTS ARE USED TO CENSOR OR RESTRICT LITERATURE AND THE ARTS

The Post Office Act, 1953, section 11.

This section uses both words 'obscene' and 'indecent' – but in practice the authorities appear to choose the word 'indecent' for the purpose of prosecutions, because this word does not carry with it the same possibility of defence as the word 'obscene'.

In the appeal judgment given against me by Reginald Seaton on 15 February, 1968, it was said:

> 'What this Court has got to consider is first of all with regard to the Post Office summons whether these photographs are indecent; that is to say, do they offend the ordinary normal person? We have absolutely no doubt whatever that they do.'

That is to say that nothing that can offend the ordinary normal person (whoever he may be) can be sent in a sealed postal packet, irrespective of the character or needs of the addressee.

I am not sure if it is intended to carry this law forward when the Post Office becomes a public corporation; but it is without question a clear breach of the concept of the privacy of the mails. The receipt by anyone of unsolicited matter is quite a different offence.

The other Acts, or common laws, which are used in practice to censor or restrict literature and the arts, with the exception of (*g*),* The Children and Young Persons Harmful Publications Act, 1955, all give effect to legislation enacted for times very different from today.

WHAT SOLID EVIDENCE THERE IS RELATING TO THE EFFECT OF LITERATURE AND THE ARTS ON BEHAVIOUR IN THE FIELDS OF SEX, VIOLENCE AND DRUGS AND THE EXTENT, IF ANY, TO WHICH PEOPLE CAN BE SAID TO BE DEPRAVED AND CORRUPTED BY LITERATURE AND THE ARTS

I said before the magistrate Leo Gradwell on 9 April, 1962, that statements like

* In the Working Party's leaflet sent to Mr Straker.

'Guinness is Good for You', and
'Players Please'

could be said to deprave and corrupt.

But the Obscene Publications Acts are not used by the authorities to suppress this type of publication. Nor are the authorities apparently concerned to examine the effect of publicity about violence and drugs, and it seems to me that it is unfortunate and misleading to associate sex with violence and drugs.

There is an examination of the term 'corrupt' by Michael Rubinstein on pages 11, 12 and 13 of the 'Censorship in the Arts' report, and of the concept of violence by Edward Bond on pages 21–24.

In the book *Sex as Gift* (published on behalf of the Scottish Churches Council) the Rev. Ian M. Fraser on page 27 writes:

> 'Knowledge of physical facts is wanting. Strange as it may seem, the venereologist and the obstetrician in the company testified that sexually experienced young people who came into their care are often substantially ignorant of the physical facts.'

And:

> 'Basic information about physical parts and functions should be given, as a right, to those whose lives it affects. In a survey of sexual attitudes and habits in certain colleges in the USA, the source of knowledge which was said to give the most help was pornographic photographs. People wanted to know what happened and how it happened.'

Although the Obscene Publications Acts are extensively used to suppress such 'pornographic photographs', which usually illustrate sexual anatomy and sexual behaviour, I am not aware that knowledge of sexual anatomy or behaviour is a vice, or harmful, or addictive. To equate the pursuit of such knowledge to other dangerous and anti-social behaviour, such as violence and drug-taking (with which some may couple drinking and smoking) is to confuse the facts, the issues and the laws.

I am not aware that crime stories, war stories, or detailed newspaper reports of atrocities, or cinema and television showings of violence, are restrained in any way by the Obscene Publications Acts or other censorship laws.

With regard to solid evidence for the corruption of people, one must take it that there is plenty, as any perusal of the *News of the*

World will show; but in the application of the Obscene Publications Acts the term 'corrupt' appears to be used in quite a different sense; it appears to mean that knowledge of sexual anatomy or sexual behaviour makes one corrupt, for there is no legislation to prevent the corruption of people in other areas of human activity. People may be corrupted by motor-cars, by gambling, by travel, by religion, by almost any enticement or activity – and people can only resist such temptation to corruption by education and self-control. Only in the field of literature and art is censorship applied to restrict the production and publication of information about human sexuality, to the extent that in this field of knowledge a great many adults grow up to be immature, physically and mentally, with the result that they are unable to behave with self-knowledge and self-control.

SUGGESTIONS FOR REFORM

Any reform of the law must be in accordance with

(*a*) the spirit of the Universal Declaration of Human Rights, and in particular within the terms of Articles 19 and 27;

(*b*) within the requirements of the European Convention on Human Rights, and in particular Article 6 (2) and Article 10 (2);

that is to say, there cannot be any presumption of a 'tendency' to commit a crime: there must be absolute proof in accordance with the rules of Criminal Law of a breach of a restriction prescribed by law.

In pursuit of this object the Freedom of Vision draft for a Freedom of Communications Bill* (which is supported by Cosmo and the Student Humanist Federation) propose that the words 'indecent' and 'obscene' be abolished as definitions of crimes in the field of artistic statement.

It is also necessary to ensure that no other crime shall be created which prevents the description in words or pictures of human anatomy or sexual behaviour.

* Superseded by Mr Hamling's Obscene Publications (Amendment) Bill.

Further as the 1964 Obscene Publications Act was in part designed to make it illegal for me to possess negatives which had been previously returned to me by order of the Divisional Court, and others, any new law should require the authorities to return all matter seized which is still in their possession.

Legislation to this effect should carry with it unilateral denunciation by HM Government of the 1923 Geneva Convention.

Appendix E.ix(a)

Obscene Publications (Amendment) Bill

Ordered to be brought in by
Mr William Hamling, Mr Raymond Fletcher,
and Mr Michael Foot

EXPLANATORY MEMORANDUM

The purpose of this Bill is to remove from the scope of the criminal law of England all common law and statutory offences relating to the publication of matter described as 'indecent' or 'obscene'.

A
BILL
TO

Amend the law relating to obscene publications — A.D. 1969

BE IT ENACTED by the Queen's most Excellent Majesty, by and with the advice and consent of the Lords Spiritual and Temporal, and Commons, in this present Parliament assembled, and by the authority of the same, as follows:

1. A person shall not be proceeded against for an offence consisting of the publication of any matter where it is of the essence of the offence that the matter is indecent or obscene. — Publication of obscenity or indecency not an offence

2. The following enactments are hereby repealed— — Repeals
(*a*) section 2 of the Vagrancy Act 1838; — 1838 c. 38
(*b*) section 42 of the Customs Consolidation Act 1876; — 1876 c. 36
(*c*) section 11(1)(*b*) of the Post Office Act 1953; — 1953 c. 36
(*d*) the Obscene Publications Act 1959; — 1959 c. 66
(*e*) the Obscene Publications Act 1964. — 1964 c. 74

3. (1) A person from whom any publication has been seized under any common law process, or under any of the Acts listed — Seized articles in section 2 of this Act, which is still held in official custody at the passing of this Act, shall be entitled to claim for the return of any such publication at any time within six months of the passing of this Act, and upon any such claim being established the detaining authorities shall return such publication to the person from whom they took it.

(2) After the expiry of six months from the date of the passing of this Act, any publication which has been seized under any common law process or under any of the Acts listed in section 2 above, and which still remains in official custody, shall be offered to the British Museum or any other public or university library at the discretion of the Secretary of State for the Home Department.

Short title, commencement and extent

4. (1) This Act may be cited as the Obscene Publications (Amendment) Act 1969.

(2) This Act shall come into operation on the expiration of one month beginning with the date of the passing thereof.

(3) This Act shall not extend to Northern Ireland, to Scotland or to Wales.

Appendix E.x

Submission to the Working Party on Obscenity Laws from Mr David Tribe

President of the National Secular Society, London, S.E.1

(1) THE WORKING OF THE OBSCENE PUBLICATIONS ACTS IN PRACTICE

If they are intended to prevent the distribution of anything that might bring a blush to a maiden aunt's cheek, they are demonstrably not working. With frequent holidaying abroad in places like Denmark that have abolished such legislation, and with the 'dirty bookshop' of Soho and the centre of other industrial cities becoming a growth industry, there can be few citizens who have never seen anything nasty in a window or have no knowledge under what counters to see something even nastier. The threat of invoking section 3 of the 1959 Act may enrich the not too scrupulous detective, and large quantities of pulp may, for all I know, end up in some judicial incinerator, but the only apparent effect is creeping inflation in the retail market as another business expense is passed on to the consuming public.

In a historical sense prosecution for obscenity links up with political intrigues and curbs on serious freedom of speech rather than with any effective or, at most periods, any strenuous effort to cut smut. Obscene was linked with seditious libel to get Wilkes, and with the Victorian industrialists' exploitation of big working class families in the absence of family planning, to get Bradlaugh. Just as the Roman Catholic *Index of Prohibited Books* gave more attention to heresy than to *erotica,* so Lord Campbell, the zealous Presbyterian who in 1857 decided the common law misdemeanour of obscene publication needed strengthening by statute law, had a sturdy background in blasphemy prosecutions. The great show trials that stand out in the mind of the general public have involved such serious creative artists as Gustave Flaubert, Havelock Ellis, James Joyce, Magnus Hirschfeld, Norman Haire, D. H. Lawrence, John Cleland, Henry Miller and

Hubert Selby Jnr, and create an impression of official philistinism. Nor, at least in the long term, have they been effective. After causing considerable, and sometimes grievous expense and worry to their authors/publishers, these attempts to suppress literature have usually failed. The net result has been the creation of a notoriety that has impaired objective literary criticism and distributed the offending volume among many who would not otherwise have heard of it.

I do not propose to comment in detail on any of the prosecutions where I have firsthand knowledge, as I imagine you will be-receiving evidence from those whose connection with the cases is more intimate. In general terms it can be said that the literary, artistic and scientific defence under section 4 of the 1959 Act seems to cut more ice with courts of appeal than with juries, with juries than with magistrates, and with creative artists than with any representatives of the law. This is hardly surprising. Not because those who have given expert defence evidence are themselves producers of 'frank' books with a professional axe to grind. On the whole they have been writers, critics and academics whose own output tends to be conservative. But they have the imagination, training and experience to assess work which, though shocking to the casual reader, cuts deep into human experience and shells out layers of truth from which our social situation germinates. Adjudicators of the law do not, by and large, have either the temperament or the background to make these assessments and should not be required to do so.

Three other points must briefly be made. Because of its immediate impact and smaller canon of established criticism and critics, visual art seems to find defence more difficult than does literature. Rule-of-thumb definitions, e.g. the ailing but still viable 'Lawrence nudes decision' that pubic hair is *ipso facto* obscene, cause special difficulties in the visual field. In the 1964 Act we have one of a growing class of statutes which make 'possession' as culpable as dissemination and represent a grave invasion of personal privacy. It is quite intolerable that wealthy prudes are able to bring private prosecution.

(2) THE EFFECT OF OTHER ACTS AND PRACTICES

(a) the common law doctrine of corruption of public morals

This rests on the assumptions that there is one universal, or at any rate national, moral code to which all classes of the community subscribe in theory if not in practice, and that this is nevertheless so unstable that a single publication may bring it into jeopardy.

Social anthropology has quite exploded the first and common experience the second.

(b) the common law conception of indecency

If this is regarded as a less heinous offence than obscenity and thus likely to attract milder penalties, it has, from the viewpoint of the defendant, the very serious drawback that it seems never to have acquired a precise legal definition and is thus almost irrefragable. He is virtually at the mercy of the physiological reactions of any puritanical policeman or postal official, customs man or magistrate.

(c) the Vagrancy Act 1824, *section* 4

This has proved a godsend for dealing with art exhibitions like that of Jim Dine. Conveniently the Act attacks 'indecent' as well as 'obscene' material. It is interesting that it is also directed against 'every person pretending or professing to tell fortunes, or using any subtle craft, means, or device, by palmistry or otherwise, to deceive or impose on any of his Majesty's subjects'; but I have yet to hear that it has been invoked to deal with any of the growing army of 'rogues and vagabonds' on the march in faith healing 'clinics', witches' covens, fortune-tellers' booths and newspaper horoscope offices.

(d) the Town Police Clauses Act 1847, *section* 28

This also embraces both indecency and obscenity. There is the revealing addition of 'profane' material, demonstrating the origin of this nineteenth century legislation in a world where religious orthodoxy jostled with sexual reticence.

(e) the Indecent Advertisements Act 1889, *sections* 3 *and* 4

Here again both indecency and obscenity flourish. The Act in fact volunteers a definition of 'indecent': 'relating to syphilis, gonorrhoea, nervous debility, or other complaint or infirmity arising from or relating to sexual intercourse'. Public urinals fall beneath its sway. So that some local authorities are liable to prosecution for daring to put up notices in toilets warning of the dangers of venereal disease and advising sufferers where to seek treatment. In such a climate of legislative snideness and secrecy it is hardly surprising that venereal diseases are proving more intractable than any other comparable ailment.

(*f*) *the Post Office Act* 1953, *section II*
Again both indecency and obscenity obtain and officials now usually take action on the easier option, indecency. This involves breaking open a communication not 'shown' to the general public but addressed from one individual to (in almost all cases) a more than willing recipient, and represents a grave invasion of privacy. To protect itself against treason a community may not accord absolute sanctity to the mail, but national survival is unlikely to be threatened by a few dirty postcards.

(*g*) *the Children and Young Persons* (*Harmful Publications*) *Act* 1955
This is undoubtedly the most difficult statute in this area to assess. Adults frequently assume harm to children on the basis that childlike innocence is being assaulted by mature comprehension, whereas true innocence lacks comprehension. Nor do I know of any real evidence that children's behaviour is more influenced than that of adults by what they read or see, and I wonder if there could be much produced more damaging than *graffiti* in school toilets. Nevertheless I am inclined to feel that it is possible to tailor sadism and perversions cynically to the juvenile market, and that if children are assumed to be especially impressionable and susceptible to good influences they might be equally responsive to bad. Even if the case against juvenile pulp be unproven it would probably be premature to repeal this statute without much more research. Though children may not be motivated to vicious activity they could be subject to psychological damage to which adults have become immune. 'Young persons' are as defined in the Children and Young Persons Act 1933, ss. 14–17. As the age of sexual consent for females and for seeing X-certificate films is sixteen, the arbitrary age of 17 definitely seems too high, but I am at present uncertain what new arbitrary age should be laid down.

(*h*) *Customs Consolidation Act* 1876
Similar observations to those in (f).

(i) Local By-Laws

This is a jungle that seems likely to defy even the Law Commissioners.

(j) any other legal sanctions

Now that the 1697 Blasphemy Act has been repealed and the offence as defined therein statute-barred, the remaining Blasphemy Laws (1547 Sacrament Act, 1548 and 1558–9 Acts of Uniformity and 1819 Criminal Libel Act) and the common law offence of blasphemy, which have in recent decades been interpreted to include an element of 'ribaldry', are akin to the Obscenity Laws in the effect on free speech.

(3) SOLID EVIDENCE OF HARMFUL EFFECTS OF LITERATURE AND THE ARTS

Despite sensational claims at and after the Moors Murder case and other *causes célèbres* there is no solid evidence that literature and the arts incite people to crimes they would not otherwise commit, though they may in certain cases suggest improved techniques. Crime fiction of this sort is, however, to the best of my knowledge, never prosecuted. *Sex Offenders: an analysis of types,* by Paul H. Gebhard and others from the Kinsey Institute, is probably the most authoritative of the many scientific papers which have stated that there is no correlation between reading habits and crime. From *a priori* psychological considerations (there is of course no solid evidence one way or the other) I would suggest that there might be more sexual offences against children, indecent exposure and the like if 'dirty old men' were unable to sublimate their feelings with hard-core pornography devoid of artistic merit.

The test of 'obscenity' in the 1959 Act, based on Cockburn's definition in R. v. *Hicklin* (1868), is 'such as to tend to deprave and corrupt persons who are likely, having regard to all relevant circumstances, to read, see or hear the matter contained or embodied in it'. This is pure speculation. No jury, judge or other lawyer imagines that he will be corrupted by the material he is obliged to assess. It is always somebody else who is held to be at risk. In all this there is a strong class bias, as cheap publications are usually deemed to be more dangerous than expensive ones.

(This was true long before children had any pocket money to speak of.) No one is ever brought into court as an awful example of depravity and corruption occasioned by the publication in the dock. It is true that at the *Last Exit to Brooklyn* trial the Rev. David Sheppard declared that he had emerged from its perusal 'not unscathed'; but his moral scars providentially healed in time for him to be appointed Bishop of Woolwich by the Queen, acting on the advice of the Prime Minister. The 1959 Act is even more illogical than its predecessors, for if publications were really able to deprave and corrupt there is no social case for considering their artistic or scholarly interest. Sex and drugs have however been abused and violence perpetrated when most people were illiterate and when the only art permitted was religious.

(4) SUGGESTIONS FOR REFORM

If the foregoing comments are valid it is clear that obscenity and indecency – and I should add blasphemy – are purely subjective and relative, have never been clearly demonstrated as harmful, and insofar as they tell us more about human beings and the hidden (perhaps dark) places of their minds and bring erotic or other pleasures to a world where misery abounds, may even be considered helpful. Censorship in the fields of the arts and communications is arbitrary and self-defeating. There is a case for penalising the publication of official secrets that are really vital to security, maliciously untrue defamatory libels, and perhaps vicious publications directed at children. Otherwise publication should be free. The common law offences of obscenity and indecency (and blasphemy) should be statute-barred and relevant statutes repealed.

Appendix E.xi

Report from Mr Keith Wedmore, M.A., LL.B.(Cantab.)

Barrister, Signatory to the Pamphlet 'Towards a Quaker View of Sex', Clerk of the Quaker Penal Affairs Committee

LITERARY CENSORSHIP

The object of censorship is to prevent corruption. The question is whether the disadvantages of censorship outweigh the advantages; so the question becomes, what are the advantages.

In a liberal society one can assume that it is not the spread of ideas that is objected to; the mischief to be attacked by censorship is apparently sexual malpractice; and the spread of violence by the contagious effect of reading about it or watching it.

To my group the first head has no real meaning. The authors of *Towards a Quaker View of Sex* were indeed concerned with the maintenance of morality, but they hold that sexual morality lies in the quality of sexual relationships, their character richness and depth, not in whether they are hetero- or homo-sexual, nor yet in the incidents of physical pleasure that characterise them. *Those* questions do not touch upon the essential worthwhileness of the relationship. That being so, I do not know what 'malpractice', in a sexual sense, *is,* or even whether it exists. I certainly cannot imagine any way of protecting people from it and I do not know whether such a notion has any meaning.

En passant I would add that neither would I expect the principles of sexual morality to be *acquired* from literature, however improving; I assume that the laws governing sound relationships are instilled from life itself and from the relationships a growing person forms with those around him, from his parents and his peer group. The arts merely provide discussion points or examples of the real world; a story is a story, and the distinction is well understood except by psychopaths, whose failure to distinguish is inherent in their condition and not set off by one particular example of it.

Violence and bullying is another matter. I think I know what that is, and that I would be affronted or terrified if the commonplaces of literature and television by way of cruelty and sudden death were translated to my daily life. But I arrive at the same conclusion for the second reason; that a story is a story, and the distinction is well understood; that children (and immature people) have their real behaviour influenced by their actual relationships; that, except for the grossly inadequate minority for whose special needs we must not try and frame our rules, we do not copy art in life; we accept it for what it is, a copy *of* life, or an expression of its desires and fantasies. Whatever nebulous case there may be for the argument that a particular incident in a book or on the screen set off a particular crime or incident – significantly most usually suggested in relation to suicide – there is a slightly stronger suggestion that we sleep and even behave better after witnessing scenes that 'get it out of our system'. But frankly my own group knew of little impressive evidence either way; so that on our impressions you would be justified in not having censorship on the simple ground that it serves no demonstrable purpose.

I agree with Professor Jackson that it may be politically impracticable to urge this, and that an acceptable compromise might be to have, as a defence, that a work has *some* merit (the degree being immaterial).

I am not sure that I agree that the suppression of pornography (meaning confessedly erotic literature) 'does not matter' since it seems to me it may serve a useful social purpose: but to keep at least the artistic or good pornography would be, frankly, better than excluding literature with erotic elements altogether; and if that is the compromise, I would accept it.

Appendix E.xii

The common law doctrines of corruption of public morals

from Mr R. J. Werry, C.B.E., B.Sc.

Headmaster of a London mixed Comprehensive School

Some years ago when I was a Head in Chelsea I drew the attention of the Youth Committee (of which I was then a member) to some photographs outside a Theatre where a revue 'Exotique' was playing. These portrayed the bayoneting by soldiers of terrified nude women and various other unsavoury things, in the neighbourhood of my school. The youth Committee put up a complaint to the then L.C.C. but the answer came that they were not pornographic, and nothing could be done. It is ridiculous, as the photographs tended to spur the young to copy violence in a sexual connotation.

More recently some small cards portraying violence, usually under torture, by Japs or other soldiery, were being given away with packets of sweets in this district (N.4). Reported, the same answer was returned via the D.O. and the Police. Similarly for a set of 52 tiny playing cards with provocative pictures of semi-nudes on the reverse side.

Another cause for concern is the way that 'sex' has crept into most advertisements, especially those on the walls of the escalators in the Tube Stations.

Nearly all contain scantily-dressed young ladies with certain parts cleverly accented by a skilled artist.

The pendulum has unfortunately swung too far now. It used to be the case that talking about sex was 'taboo'. Now the interest is deliberately awakened in children from 9 onwards in comics, posters, television, plays, the Press, the shops – everywhere.

I have stopped from my Library here the supply of some magazines dealing with art and the cinema because I considered them unsuitable, though they contain much that is good and informative about current work. In the case of theatrical magazines, I sometimes feel obliged to remove from them on arrival subject matter which I consider quite unsuitable for adolescent minds. I am defeated in this unfortunately by the kindness of wholesale newsagents. I have been into a Youth Club and seen a whole pile of unsold magazines containing such material, all unexpurgated.

Appendix F.i

Text of Laws indirectly affecting Obscenity

(1) THE VAGRANCY ACT, 1824

Section 4

Persons committing certain offences shall be deemed rogues and vagabonds and may be imprisoned for three months with hard labour . . . Every person committing any of the offences hereinbefore mentioned, after having been convicted as an idle and disorderly person; every person pretending or professing to tell fortunes, or using any subtle craft, means, or device, by palmistry or otherwise, to deceive and impose on any of his Majesty's subjects; every person wandering abroad and lodging in any barn or outhouse, or in any deserted or unoccupied building, or in the open air, or under a tent, or in any cart or waggon . . . and not giving a good account of himself or herself; every person wilfully exposing to view, in any street, road, highway, or public place, any obscene print, picture, or other indecent exhibition; every person wilfully, openly, lewdly, and obscenely exposing his person . . . with intent to insult any female; every person wandering abroad, and endeavouring by the exposure of wounds or deformities to obtain or gather alms; every person going about as a gatherer or collector of alms, or endeavouring to procure charitable contributions of any nature or kind, under any false or fraudulent pretence; . . . every person having in his or her custody or possession any picklock key, crow, jack, bit, or other implement, with intent feloniously to break into any dwelling house, warehouse, coach-house, stable, or outbuilding, or being armed with any gun, pistol, hanger, cutlass, bludgeon, or other offensive weapon, or having upon him or her any instrument, with intent to commit any felonious act; every person being found in or upon any dwelling house, warehouse, coach-house, stable, or outhouse, or in any enclosed yard, garden, or area, for any unlawful purpose; every suspected person or reputed thief, frequenting any river, canal, or navigable stream, dock or basin, or any quay, wharf, or warehouse near or adjoining thereto, or any street, highway, or avenue leading thereto, or any place of public resort, or any avenue leading thereto, or any street (or any highway or any place adjacent to a street or highway) with intent to commit felony; and every person apprehended as an idle and disorderly person, and violently resisting any constable, or other peace officer so apprehending him or her, and being subsequently convicted of the offence for which he or she shall have been so apprehended; shall be deemed a rogue and vagabond, within the true intent and meaning of this Act; and it shall be lawful for any justice of the peace to commit such offender (being thereof convicted before him by the confession of such offender, or by the evidence on oath of one or more credible witness or witnesses) to the house of correction, there to be kept to hard labour for any time not exceeding three calendar months; and every such pick-lock, key, crow, jack, bit, and other implement, and every such gun, pistol, hanger, cutlass, bludgeon, or other offensive weapon, and every such instrument as aforesaid, shall, by the conviction of the offender, become forfeited to the King's Majesty.

(2) THE VAGRANCY ACT, 1838

Section 2

Persons exposing obscene prints, etc. in shop windows liable on conviction to punishment . . . Every person who shall wilfully expose or cause to be exposed to public view in the window or other part of any shop or other building situate in any street, road, highway, or public place, any obscene print, picture, or other indecent exhibition, shall be deemed to have wilfully exposed such obscene print, picture, or other indecent exhibition to public view within the intent and meaning of the said Act, and shall accordingly be liable to be proceeded against, and on conviction to be punished, under the provisions of the said Act.

(3) TOWN POLICE CLAUSES ACT, 1847

Section 28

Penalty on persons committing any of the offences herein named. Every person who in any street, to the obstruction, annoyance, or danger of the residents or passengers, commits any of the

following offences, shall be liable to a penalty not exceeding forty shillings for each offence, or, in the discretion of the justice before whom he is convicted, may be committed to prison, there to remain for a period not exceeding fourteen days; and any constable or other officer appointed by virtue of this or the special Act shall take into custody, without warrant, and forthwith convey before a justice, any person who within his view commits any such offence; (that is to say) . . .
Every person who publicly offers for sale or distribution, or exhibits to public view any profane, indecent, or obscene book, paper, print, drawing, painting, or representation, or sings any profane or obscene song or ballad, or uses any profane or obscene language . . .

(4) EXTRACT FROM CUSTOMS CONSOLIDATION ACT, 1876

Section 42
The goods enumerated and described in the following table of prohibitions and restrictions inward are hereby prohibited to be imported or brought into the United Kingdom . . . and if any goods so enumerated and described shall be imported or brought into the United Kingdom . . . such goods shall be forfeited and may be destroyed or otherwise disposed of as the Commissioners of Customs may direct . . .

A TABLE OF PROHIBITIONS AND RESTRICTIONS INWARDS
Goods prohibited to be imported.
Indecent or obscene prints, paintings, photographs, books, cards, lithographic or other engravings or any other indecent or obscene articles.

(5) THE INDECENT ADVERTISEMENTS ACT, 1889

Section 3
Summary proceedings against persons affixing, etc., indecent or obscene pictures or printed or written matter. Whoever affixes to or inscribes on any house, building, wall, hoarding, gate, fence, pillar, post, board, tree, or any other thing whatsoever so as to be visible to a person being in or passing along any street, public highway, or footpath and whoever affixes to or inscribes on any public

urinal, or delivers or attempts to deliver or exhibits to any inhabitant or to any person being in or passing along any street, public highway, or footpath, or throws down the area of any house, or exhibits to public view in the window of any house or shop, any picture or printed or written matter which is of an indecent or obscene nature, shall, on summary conviction in manner provided by the Summary Jurisdiction Acts, be liable to a penalty not exceeding forty shillings, or, in the discretion of the court, to imprisonment for any term not exceeding one month, with or without hard labour.

Section 4
Summary proceedings against persons sending others to do the acts punishable under s. 3. Whoever gives or delivers to any other person any such pictures, or printed or written matter mentioned in section three of this Act, with the intent that the same, or some one or more thereof, should be affixed, inscribed, delivered, or exhibited as therein mentioned, shall, on conviction in manner provided by the Summary Jurisdiction Acts, be liable to a penalty not exceeding five pounds, or, in the discretion of the Court, to imprisonment for any term not exceeding three months, with or without hard labour.

(6) POST OFFICE ACT, 1953

Section 11
Prohibition on sending by post of certain articles.

(1) A person shall not send or attempt to send or procure to be sent a postal packet which . . .

(*b*) encloses any indecent or obscene print, painting, photograph, lithograph, engraving, cinematograph film, book, card or written communication, or any indecent or obscene article whether similar to the above or not; or

(*c*) has on the packet, or on the cover thereof, any words, marks or designs which are grossly offensive or of an indecent or obscene character.

(2) If any person acts in contravention of the foregoing sub-section, he shall be liable on summary conviction to a fine not

exceeding ten pounds or on conviction on indictment to imprisonment for a term not exceeding twelve months.

(3) Post Office regulations may be made for preventing the sending or delivery by post of any such articles as are mentioned in paragraph (*b*) or (*c*) of subsection (1) of this section or of any postal packet having thereon, or on the cover thereof, any words, marks or designs of a libellous character.

(4) The detention in the Post Office of any postal packet on the grounds of a contravention of this section or of any regulations made thereunder shall not exempt the sender thereof from any proceedings which might have been taken if the packet had been delivered in due course of post.

NOTE. The Postmaster-General is by section 16 subsection 1 of the 1961 Post Office Act empowered to act by regulations made under Statutory Instrument instead of obtaining a warrant from the Treasury.

(7) THE CHILDREN AND YOUNG PERSONS (HARMFUL PUBLICATIONS) ACT, 1955

Section 1

Works to which this Act applies. This Act applies to any book, magazine or other like work which is of a kind likely to fall into the hands of children or young persons and consists wholly or mainly of stories told in pictures (with or without the addition of written matter), being stories portraying—

(*a*) the commission of crimes; or
(*b*) acts of violence or cruelty; or
(*c*) incidents of a repulsive or horrible nature;

in such a way that the work as a whole would tend to corrupt a child or young person into whose hands it might fall.

Section 2

Penalty for printing, publishing, selling, etc., works to which this Act applies. (1) A person who prints, publishes, sells or lets on hire a work to which this Act applies, or has any such work in his possession for the purpose of selling it or letting it on hire, shall be guilty of an offence and liable, on summary conviction, to imprisonment for a term not exceeding four months or to a fine not exceeding one hundred pounds or both:

Provided that, in any proceedings taken under this subsection against a person in respect of selling or letting on hire a work or of having it in his possession for the purpose of selling it or letting it on hire, it shall be a defence for him to prove that he had not examined the contents of the work and had no reasonable cause to suspect that it was one to which this Act applies.

(2) A prosecution for an offence under this section shall not, in England or Wales, be instituted except by, or with the consent of, the Attorney General.

Section 3

Power to search for, and dispose of, works to which this Act applies and articles for printing them. (1) Where, upon an information being laid before a justice of the peace that a person has, or is suspected of having, committed an offence under the last foregoing section with respect to a work (hereinafter in this subsection referred to as 'the relevant work'), the justice issues a summons directed to that person requiring him to answer to the information or issues a warrant to arrest that person, that or any other justice, if satisfied by written information substantiated on oath that there is reasonable ground for suspecting that the said person has in his possession or under his control—

(*a*) any copies of the relevant work or any other work to which this Act applies; or

(*b*) any plate prepared for the purpose of printing copies of the relevant work or any other work to which this Act applies or any photographic film prepared for that purpose;

may grant a search warrant authorising any constable named therein to enter (if necessary by force) any premises specified in the warrant and any vehicle or stall used by the said person for the purpose of trade or business and to search the premises, vehicle or stall and seize any of the following things which the constable finds therein or thereon, that is to say—

(i) any copies of the relevant work and any copies of any other work which the constable has reasonable cause to believe to be one to which this Act applies; and

(ii) any plate which the constable has reasonable cause to believe to have been prepared for the purpose of printing copies of any such work as is mentioned in paragraph (i) of this subsection and any photographic film which he has reasonable cause to believe to have been prepared for that purpose.

(2) The court by or before which a person is convicted of an offence under the last foregoing section with respect to a work may order any copies of that work and any plate prepared for the purpose of printing copies of that work or photographic film prepared for that purpose, being copies which have, or a plate or film which has, been found in his possession or under his control, to be forfeited.

Provided that an order made under this subsection by a magistrates' court or, on appeal from a magistrates' court, by a court of quarter sessions shall not take effect until the expiration of the ordinary time within which an appeal in the matter of the proceedings in which the order was made may be lodged (whether by giving notice of appeal or applying for a case to be stated for the opinion of the High Court) or, where such an appeal is duly lodged, until the appeal is finally decided or abandoned.

Appendix F.ii

Denmark's Legislation concerning Pornography

Received from the Press and Cultural Department of the Royal Danish Embassy in London

In Denmark as in many other countries, legislation has for many years existed to restrict the production and sale of pornography.

Danish governments have in the past signed international conventions for the control of pornography.

In recent years, from about the mid-1950's, however, the wider use of sexual subjects by serious artists in their work posed increasingly difficult questions concerning intent. Certain works could be considered to have artistic merit, but could also be termed obscene under the generally accepted standards of the day.

The general practice of courts in Denmark at this stage was that descriptions of sexual matters could not be considered criminal pornography within the meaning of the relevant legislation where the description had an intention beyond the pornographic, and which also came from an author with literary position.

This interpretation, which concerned only written pornography, came under an increasingly widespread public debate in the early 1960's. In the field of pornographic pictures, a somewhat similar attitude led to a general ruling that straightforward representations of nudity, without special sexual overtones, were acceptable.

A turning point came when the 200 year old book *Fanny Hill* was published in Denmark in 1964. The publisher was prosecuted but acquitted.

In an effort to establish an interpretation of obscenity, the *Fanny Hill* case was taken to the Supreme Court, where the acquittal was upheld.

This and similar cases, and the widespread public discussion that accompanied them, led to a rapid rise in the number of books of pornographic content sold in Denmark. It became almost a sport for publishers to issue a book, and sell the entire issue before the police could obtain a seizure order. For the public, a confiscation became little more than extra advertising, and proof that a book fulfilled its promise of being hard core pornography.

To end a situation that was becoming intolerable, the Ministry of Justice in December 1964 requested the Permanent Criminal Law committee to consider the existing legislation concerning pornography and recommend changes.

The report by the committee was completed in June 1966. Three committee members recommended that the production, publication and circulation of obscene books, magazines, etc., should no longer come under the criminal code, while the fourth member wished the prohibition to be maintained.

All four members felt it would not be advisable to remove restrictions on pictorial pornography at the same time that restrictions on written pornography were removed.

In agreement with this report, the Danish Folketing (Parliament) in the spring of 1967 approved changes in the Act, and removed all restrictions on written pornography.

Summarizing developments since then, the present Minister of Justice, Mr Knud Thestrup, said in an article published in a newspaper here that soon after these restrictions were removed 'difficulties began to develop in selling pornographic books. Publishers who printed the books tried to counter falling sales by price reductions, but even this was not successful. Today there is a far smaller sale of such books than there was when the publication of written pornography was punishable.'

Instead, sales of pictorial pornography increased considerably. Police action was taken in many cases, but the courts had difficulty in reaching a firm interpretation of the legislation.

Justice Minister Thestrup commented on this that 'in my view, the administration should not censor the reading matter of adults. I also feel – and here I am supported by many experts – that pornographic books and pictures very quickly become boring and distasteful to adults with a normal sexual life. On this basis, I have concluded that the increase in pictorial pornography which came when restrictions on written pornography were removed was to a considerable degree the result of curiosity about what is forbidden, and a desire to go against a prohibition that the general public did not consider was sufficiently well-founded. This can no doubt be considered a common human trait.'

Sociologists and others in Denmark had expressed considerable doubt that restrictions could in any way have a beneficial effect, he noted.

'On this basis,' the Minister said, 'I consider that it would be most correct to remove the restrictions on pictorial pornography – on condition it is possible to hinder offensive window displays, and sample advertising to the general public. This condition can be met by an alteration of city ordinances.'

'There remains a further question – our attitude towards other countries. Will our reputation abroad be that of a breeding ground for pornography or similar? It can hardly be denied that in many other countries Denmark is already considered as something in this direction. Elimination of the punishment for pornography will hardly bring any change in this. One may however hope for a change in this attitude if the aggressive window displays, which are a main cause of comment, disappear from our towns.'

Already, Denmark has withdrawn from the International Convention on Suppression of Trade in Obscene Publications, which was concluded in Geneva on 12 September, 1923, and ratified by Denmark in 1930.

For films, the Danish Folketing is at present considering legislation that will completely remove all censorship on films for adults, but at the same time set a two-tier restriction for children. Censors would be able to judge a film as not suitable for children under 12 years or under 16 years – or approve it for exhibition without limitation, with or without certain cuts.

The text of the bill notes that members of the censorship committee must have educational or psychological training. They are appointed for a 4 year term, and must not be over 60 years of age. The bill also provides for formation of a five member Censorship Appeal Board, again with stress on the educational or psychological background of its members.

The text of the Danish Criminal Code, Sect. 234, which concerns pornography is as follows in the new version after the change made in 1967:

'Any person who

(i) offers or hands over to any person under eighteen years of age obscene pictures or objects; or who

(ii) publishes or circulates or, for such purpose, produces or imports obscene pictures or objects; or who

(iii) arranges for any public lecture, performance or exhibition of an obscene nature;

shall be liable to a fine or to simple detention or, in aggravating circumstances, to imprisonment for any term not exceeding six months.'

Appendix F.iii

Paper from The Danish Forensic Medicine Council to The Danish Penal Code Council

published in The Penal Code Council Report on Penalty for Pornography, *report no.* 435, *Copenhagen* 1966, *p.* 78–80

In reply to the Penal Code Council's question of 25 May 1965, the Council would refer you as an introduction to its two earlier replies of 28 December 1956 and 11 May 1962, both connected with the matter of infringement of the Penal Code paragraph 234. In both these replies the Council states that it is impossible to make any authoritative statement on the effect on the minds of adults and children that the reading of 'obscene' writings or the viewing of 'obscene' films, pictures or objects may have, because no scientific experiments exist to throw any light on the said problem. Nor, at the present time, do there exist, as far as the Council is aware, scientific publications explicitly answering the question of the effect of pornographic writing, films, etc. on the minds of adults and children.

The problem in question is further complicated by the fact that no clear definition of the legal concept of 'obscene' writings has yet been given. Nor is there widespread agreement about what constitutes perverted sexual behaviour. The concept of perversion is difficult to define. It includes a mass of more or less deviating sexual activity, some of which enters into normal sexual behaviour; but it is commonly known that sexual norms, and thus what may be considered as deviations therefrom, vary considerably both from age to age and among different cultural circles, and within the same cultural circles these norms vary to a certain degree with different social and cultural structures.

Thus considerations of a medical nature will only in a limited sense be able to act as a guide as far as the question raised by the Penal Code Council is concerned. With the reservation that there is a lack of dependable scientific research to support them, the Council will answer the matter in question as follows:

The question whether there is any causal link between the reading of pornographic books or writings and sexual crimes has been the subject of research by several recognized criminologists. Thus Sheldon and Eleanor Glueck (in *Predicting Delinquency and Crime,* Harvard University Press, 1959) carried out an analysis of criminal factors in 1,000 boys who had been found guilty of juvenile offences. The researchers could not, in any case, prove that the reading of pornographic or erotic literature had been a contributory factor in the committing of crimes. Dr Karl Christiansen (at the meeting of the Penal Code Council, 3 May 1965) stated that, as far as he knew, there was absolutely no scientific basis for attributing to the reading of 'obscene' writing any of the offences mentioned in clause 24 of the Penal Code. Dr le Maire (*Legal Castration in the Light of Criminal Law,* Disputats, 1946), going through a large number of criminal cases concerning sexual offences, showed that there was really no information to be found to prove that the reading of erotica or pornography could be assumed to have had any significance in the committed offences.

Thus the Council have no knowledge of scientific research which can be taken as proof that the reading of the specific writings in question, either by adults or children, contributes to infringements of the Penal Code by the parties in question.

Whether such reading or looking at 'obscene' pictures or films can be said to influence the sexual leanings of adults, the Council can state that it is commonly known in medical science that sexual leanings are fixed at an early age, probably around 5–6 years old, and are in any case completely established by the end of puberty. It is therefore hardly likely that the reading of 'obscene' writings or the sight of films, etc. will change the sexual leanings of an adult person.

Most people will be sexually stimulated by explicit erotic and pornographic description, unless the pornographic description is so coarse and unaesthetic as to be immediately repulsive to sexually normal people. The writers of such works aim at influencing the emotions erotically. This kind of sexual stimulation cannot in itself have any harmful effect on the reader. It can lead to sexual activity either with others or in the form of masturbation. As far as adult individuals are concerned, there are no bases for assuming any detrimental influence therefrom, either on the development of the person's mind or on their attitude to sexual activity. It is a matter of whether this sexual stimulation arises from pornographic writing of the type describing normal or deviating sexual activity, or whether it arises from the sight of 'obscene' films, pictures, etc. displaying normal or deviating sexual scenes or activity.

Before we approach the question of the possible effect on children and young people, it must be remarked that the Council is of the opinion that those people who buy and read pornographic books and procure 'obscene' pictures and films are, for the vast majority, middle-aged and elderly men who seek sexual stimulation in this way. We can leave any detrimental effect completely out as far as pre-school age children are concerned, since the means in question here (pornographic literature, pictures and films) will hardly be understood by the child as pornography. Early childhood may be assumed to have great importance in the psycho-sexual development of the child, but here it is emotional experiences within the family in connection with the child's role as a boy or a girl and the identification with parents and brothers and sisters which will determine this development.

By school age children will apparently often show an interest in and be able to a large extent to 'understand' pornography; but the sexual role of the child is by now so fixed that one can scarcely reckon with further means, such as pornography, changing the sexual leanings of the child in any essential respect. Nor is there any reason to suppose that such further influence can cause the development of neurosis or other mental suffering in the child.

At puberty sexual experience acquires such a strong and socio-psychological quality that the question of the influence of pornography becomes more relevant than during actual childhood. The personality of the young person is insecure and undefined, open to influences from different directions, and fantasy is easily stimulated in those spheres aimed at by pornography. It must be stressed that at this age also the personal influence of contemporaries, parents and teachers and so on is essential for the general mental and psychosexual development of the young person. The effect of pornography will consist above all in the stimulation of sexual inclinations in the already existing direction and it is therefore doubtful whether pornography can change the direction of sexual inclinations.

In conclusion from the above, it can be stated as far as children and young people are concerned, that the experience of child and juvenile psychiatry gives no basis for assuming that pornography has any detrimental effect of significance which may cause sickness or abnormality. It is personal impressions, relations with individual people, and not coarse, external means which determine the development of a psychosexual nature in children and young people.

In the Council's view it is rather doubtful whether the reading of erotica and pornography can have a beneficial effect. In the following cases a beneficial effect may possibly result: neurotic, sexually shy people may, from the reading of very free, even pornographic descriptions of *normal* sexual activity be freed from some of their apprehension connected with sex and thereby attain a freer and less frustrated attitude to the sexual side of life. On the other hand, it cannot be ruled out that books about sadism, masochism or other perversions may increase apprehension in people who are very strongly neurotic about sex. For people who are beset by different sexual perversions, it is not unlikely that reading descriptions of perverted sexual activity will give them satisfaction through fantasy in connection with masturbation. Their deviating sexual tendencies are thereby neutralized and they thus manage to stop living out their possible perverse sexual impulses which might possibly lead them into punishable offences either humiliating or debasing for themselves. In contrast it cannot be ruled out that the effect of sexual excitement can lead uncertainly sexually-oriented young people and adults into a display of perversion.

To sum up, the Council will hereafter state that, as far as the Council is aware, no scientific experiments exist which can lay a basis for the assumption that pornography or 'obscene' pictures and films contribute to the committing of sexual offences by normal adults or young people. On the basis of psychiatric and child-psychiatric experience it can neither be assumed that sexual leanings, the development of personality, and the ordinary attitude to sex and to ethical-sexual norms either in children or adults, can be detrimentally affected by the means in question (pornographic literature, pictures and films). It is doubtful whether these can have a beneficial effect on sexually shy, neurotic people, but it cannot be completely ruled out. This statement holds good regardless of whether the pornographic writings, pictures, etc. are of normal or sexually perverted content.

Finally it is stated that the Forensic Medicine Council is quite well aware that the question of whether section 234 of the Penal Code should be changed or annulled is also subject to other opinions than medical ones.

All members of the Council's psychiatric department and medical superintendent Kaj Tolstrup MD have taken part in the discussion of this report.